Yours Affectionately
R. Faurot

THE PILGRIM'S PROGRESS

FROM THE

CITY OF DESTRUCTION TO THE CELESTIAL CITY OF REFUGE, FROM A GOSPEL STAND-POINT

CONTAINING

Interviews with Sectarians on Various Topics.

BY RANDAL FAUROT, V.D.M.

Thus saith the Lord, Stand ye in the ways and see and ask for the old paths, where is the good way, and walk therein, and ye shall find rest to your soul.—JER. vi. 16.

PHILADELPHIA:
RANDAL FAUROT, V.D.M.
1864.

PHILADELPHIA:
STEREOTYPED AND PRINTED BY ALFRED MARTIEN.

PREFACE.

It seems, at first sight, unnecessary to multiply words, on subjects not only seemingly exhausted, but dressed in *charms*, that must throw all rivals into the shade; but the fact that a subject so important, as that of directing a soul, lost in the wilderness of sin, to its Father's home in heaven, has been treated in enticing allegory and interesting style, by minds so filled with Calvinistic or Arminian theories (as Bunyan's and Shrubsole's, etc.), that it gives a false and fatal coloring to points where sinners and saints also need clear light, forms my only reason for this attempt.

For I shall only attempt to follow, with my little hand car, along the track which they have graded, removing the rotten and crooked *sleepers* of unscriptural notions, and supplying their place with tried Gospel ones. And, instead of making human experience, however bright, the standard or ground of assurance, I shall endeavor to make the Gospel the standard and the Divine Promises the only ground of assurance. If different experiences should be met with on the journey, as they doubtless will be, the final appeal will be "to the law and the testimony, if they speak not according to this word, it is because there is no light in them." (Isa. viii. 20.)

Let no one suppose because fictitious names are assumed, therefore, all is fictitious. These names I shall endeavor to select as representatives of parties, or views, giving the utmost diligence to represent them faithfully. So critics are relieved from the labor of showing that it follows others, since this is all it aims to do.

R. F.

CONTENTS.

THE PILGRIM'S PROGRESS.

CHAPTER I.

THE WORLD AS IT WAS AND IS—GOD'S MANNER OF AWAKENING SINNERS—ONE SETS OUT ON A JOURNEY.

For even hereunto were ye called, because Christ also suffered for us, leaving us an example that ye should follow his steps.—1 PETER ii. 21.

ONE of the secrets of eternity after revolving cycles stood out in the form of a globe, gradually emerging from the enveloping clouds and smoke of its primordial existence, destined to be the stage of strange scenes, for no sooner did rational inhabitants appear, as the crowning furniture and responsible "lord of the fowl and the brute," than they soon appeared in rebellion against the original proprietor and rightful governor, under the lead of Prince Apolyon, the mortal enemy of the Prince of Peace. This rebel tyrant (for such he soon proved to be) succeeded in filling the hearts of the inhabitants with bitter opposition and hatred to their rightful King (Eph. ii. 2), although he still kept up his protection over them (Matt. v. 45), and sent them constant supplies, and continually sent *messengers*, to persuade them of his good intentions.

But having entertained these evil and rebellious thoughts toward their King, they were ashamed to be seen by him (Gen. iii. 8), and so they fled away from the beautiful country he had fitted up with most astonishing taste and splendor (Gen. ii. 8), and, although wild briers entangled their path, and serpents hissed at them, and the wild beasts howled around as the clouds grew thicker and obscured the light of the sun, and awful thunders muttered in the heavens above, while anon vivid flashes of lightning shot athwart this gathering darkness, and at times the very earth trembled as though it were about to fall to pieces. At length they came to a large plain, and here they began to build a large city, although the soil was very sandy and barren, and there was no living water, save what was brought in the hands of a few men, of very pleasing appearance, who had discovered a living spring, and who offered to supply the city so abundantly that none should ever want for water. (John iv. 13.) But the inhabitants kept on building, and making little cisterns, that held a scanty supply of water, and then dried and cracked, and let it all out (Jer. ii. 13), so that the people suffered greatly for the want of water.

This city they named "Destruction," and the palace of their King they called Carnality. (Phil. iii. 19.) The chief of officers that stood around the King were, the Hon. Lust-of-the-Flesh, Secretary of State; Hon. Lust-of-the-eye, Secretary of Foreign Affairs; Hon. Pride-of-Life, Secretary of War; Hon. Mr. Appetite, Secretary of the Interior. Under the shrewd management of these, many provinces were added to their dominion—such as the provinces of Sensuality, Pride, Deceit, Ambition, Inner-light, etc.

Things seemed to be moving on pleasantly. They had contrived to satisfy their present thirst by scant supplies from the province of Inner-light, Self-conceit, and Stupidity, and this, with their gas-lamps and street-cars, helped them to get on pretty well; and with their ball-rooms, theatres, saloons, enabled them to pass away the time, forgetful of a gathering storm that was soon to overtake and destroy their city.

A small society was formed, of the most intelligent citizens, for the improvement of education and morals, and called *ouranographers*. These men built observatories, and wrote out what they saw in the heavens. (1 Pet. i. 11.) They discovered this coming storm, and many other strange things which they put in their book. (2 Pet. i. 15.) One day a citizen who had been in the habit of carrying burdens for the various public houses, and houses of entertainment in the city, came across one of the books, written by these men, and as he read, his burdens seemed to grow heavier; indeed, his knees began to tremble, and he felt as though he could not stand. He had agreed to act as porter for these houses, and he knew that they would not readily let him off, and he felt certain from the calculations of these wise men, that he would not have any more than time, if ever so diligent, to settle up his affairs, set his house in order, and leave the city before the storm came upon it (1 Pet. iv. 7); nay, without great haste (Heb. vi. 18), to get to a place of safety, so he resolved to go at once to his employers and tell them that he could serve them no longer. But they at first mocked him, and this only made him the more resolute. (Acts xiii. 48.) Then they began to reason with him, saying, you have been reading that foolish book published by the ouranographers, and it has frightened you. (Acts xxvi. 24.) Look around, do you see any signs of such a storm? (2 Pet. iii. 9.) But putting his fingers in his ears, he turned away from them, and resolved that he would get ready and leave the city, and see if he could not find a place of safety, for he read that there was such a place not far off (2 Tim. ii. 11), yet he did not know exactly which road to take, since there were so many leading out of the city; and although he had been out on most of them a little way, yet having never before heard of the city of Refuge, he did not know which led to that. At first he thought he would seek out the wise men. But then as he saw his neighbors standing along, some of whom he knew to be honest and acquainted with some of the roads, he concluded he would turn aside and inquire of some of them peradventure they might tell him which of the many was the best road.

CHAPTER II.

THE POOR TREMBLING PILGRIM SETS OUT—FORGETS HIS MOTTO, AND TURNS TO CONSULT HIS NEIGHBOR'S.

Immediately I conferred not with flesh and blood.—GAL. i. 16.

ALTHOUGH this poor man had read in this same book of others in a similar situation with himself, and had even read what one did (see motto) and how he succeeded (2 Tim. iv. 8), yet in his anxiety and haste he forgot all this, and went to talk to his neighbor.

He had not gone far before he saw a man with his head shaven and exposed, with downcast mien and strange dress; in his left hand he held a string of beads suspending a little cross, his right hand upheld a sword.

PILGRIM. Sir, from your appearance and age, I judge that you are a man of much note, and have lived a long time in this city.

PRIEST. Yes, sir, I have dwelt in this city almost from the days of Paul. (2 Thess. ii. 7.) My business is to direct those who wish to escape from its destruction, and to protect them in their journey to a place of safety.

PILGRIM. Oh! how glad I am to meet you. I am a poor pilgrim. I have just heard that this city was soon to be destroyed, and I am anxious to escape, if you can direct me.

PRIEST. I judge from the looks of the book in your hand, that you have fallen in with a perverted copy of the reports of the *ouranographists*. Sir, that copy was published by evil men, which has caused much needless alarm, not only to you, but many others, and even if it were a correct copy, like ours, (Douay) you could not understand it without the explanation of the Catholic church!

PILGRIM. Well, as I am but a poor pilgrim, if you can only give me clear and definite directions, I am anxious to be on my journey for I cannot rest.

PRIEST. You may have read even in that corrupt copy of yours, that the Prince Immanuel, when about to leave this city of Destruction, to go into a far country (Luke xix. 12), to receive his crown and establish a place of refuge (Jo. xiv. 2), said, "I give to you the keys of the kingdom." (Matt. xvi. 19.) These keys you see hanging to my girdle are those very keys, and you have well done that you have come to me, for I am the only one that can open the gate leading into the highway going up to this city. (Matt. xvi. 19.)

PILGRIM. Oh! sir, do not keep me in suspense; I am anxious to be on my journey.

PRIEST. Young man, you seem to be too eager, too much agitated. There are many things for you to learn.

PILGRIM. True, sir. You see this great load upon my back. Oh! I must get rid of this or I shall die, and to be rid of this seems to me necessary before I start.

PRIEST. Yes, but that load cannot be fully taken off; it will keep growing, because it is a part of your very nature, but these beads and this cross show that I can reduce its size, and then keep it so small that with great effort, and a proper faith you can carry it along with you, till you arrive at the city of Refuge.

PILGRIM. Oh! wretched man that I am, who shall deliver me from this burden? Sir, my soul is exceeding sorrowful; I have just read in this book that unless I am born again (Jo. iii. 5), I cannot get into this city of Refuge. What can this mean? I do not understand it.

PRIEST. No, nor can you unless you hear the holy Catholic church. God said to the church, "He that heareth you heareth me," that is, as St. Origin saith, "They who teach the word according to the church are the prophets of God." Now this church was organized before that garbled collection, of a few of the Apostolic Fathers' writings, which you call the New Testament, was made, at which time the Ancient Traditions were made, by which alone these writings can be interpreted. Here we understand, from these sacred and infallible traditions, many things not mentioned by the apostles in these writings, such as the baptism of infants, which St. Augustine says "could not be believed at all were it not for these Apostolic Traditions;" so of "prayers, sacrifices and alms for the dead," with the "invocation of saints, the sacrament of *Confirmation, Eucharist*, or *Real Body and Blood, Penance and Extreme Unction*," (Balemy's His. p. 193), together with the infallibility of the

Holy Mother church. All this you must believe, and commit your soul to the holy vicar of Christ, the Pope, who is the infallible head of the church on earth.

PILGRIM. But I also read in this book not to call any man Lord. (Matt. xxiii. 8.) And that all things necessary to life were given here. (2 Pet. i. 3.) That secret things belong to God, and nothing but revealed things belong to us (Deut. xxix. 29); that none should desire to know what is not written (1 Cor. iv. 6), and that he that would believe with all his heart on the Lord Jesus (Rom. x. 10), and commit their souls to Him by well-doing, as into the hands of a faithful Creator (1 Pet. iv. 19), should be saved (Mark xvi. 16), and he that did not should be damned. Hence, sir, my mind is now distracted, this burden increased, and my strength fast giving way. What shall I do! What shall I do!

PRIEST. Son, seest thou that beautiful palace standing upon seven hills? (Rev. xvii. 3). That is the true church, enter her portals, give yourself no further trouble about that burden, be of good cheer, you will there find the great *under shepherd,* who will henceforth take care of your spiritual concerns, and you will find innumerable saints and martyrs ready to intercede for you. Go seek their aid and all will be well.

PILGRIM. As I told you my eyes are getting dim by reason of the fog arising before me (2 Jo. 7), and I cannot see the palace clearly. Is that it surrounded by those gloomy walls? What mean those dreadful instruments of torture? Do my eyes deceive me, or is that blood flowing down yon sewer? (Rev. xvii. 6.) Whose are those dead bodies that lay strewed around? What sound is that as of helpless females shrieking for protection from the ravisher of her virtue, and ruiner of her peace? Is that indeed a place of safety? I read that there is but one Mediator. (1 Tim. ii. 5.) Then what can martyred saints, or even angels, do for me, for there is but one name given under heaven whereby we can be saved. (Acts iv. 12.) What shall I do, then, to be saved. (Acts xiii. 30.)

PRIEST. Young man, you are not the only one that has been ruined by heresy. The holy church, which alone is of authority, directs that you pray for aid to the "*Holy Mary, mother of God, virgin of virgins, St. Michael, St. Gabriel, St. Raphael,* all holy angels and arch-angels, all holy orders of blessed spirits, *St. John the Baptist, St. Joseph,* all holy patriarchs and prophets, *St. Paul, St. Peter, St. Andrew, St. James, St. Philip, St. Bartholomew, St. Mathew, St. Barnaby, St. Luke, St. Mark,* all holy evangelists and disciples of our Lord, all holy doctors, all holy innocents, all holy martyrs, all holy bishops and confessors, all holy priests and Levites, all holy monks and hermits, all holy virgins and widows, all holy saints of God" (Bellamy p. 201), and then you may be saved.

At this poor Pilgrim became nearly frantic. Another and strange fear was added to his former trouble. Just then he thought he saw a monk

(Luther) bursting out of one of the gates of the palace, and breaking off the chains from his hands and feet, and pointing with violent gesticulations to the palace, run towards poor Pilgrim, uttering fierce imprecations, among which he heard, "Anti-christ, *mother of harlots, abominations*," etc., whereat the priest, livid with rage, turned away muttering, "You will not behave yourselves till more of you are burnt," whereupon Pilgrim, not understanding all this, accosted the new comer.

PILGRIM. Pray, sir, can you tell me what I must do to get to a place of safety? I learn from this book that if I remain here I must die, and this city will soon be destroyed by fire. Is there a place of safety near at hand; if so, which road must I take to reach it?

SOLEFIDIAN. (For such was the man's name—*faith alone.*) What can you do? Do you not see, sir, that your garments are all tattered so that they do not hide your bruised and mangled limbs? Is it not clear that one so diseased as you are from the crown of the head to the sole of the feet, must be utterly incapable of thinking a good thought, or taking one step in getting to a place of safety?

PILGRIM. Wo is me, for I am undone! Would that I had never been born! But, sir, I have just heard that there is a Physician in yonder palace that can heal these bruises and pretty much remove this burden. Can he afford me any protection or relief?

SOLEFIDIAN. Sir, he is nothing but *anti-christ.* True he sets in the temple of God (2 Thes. ii. 4), and even grants the indulgence of pardon for sins before they are committed, but it is all false, none can forgive sins but God only; neither has man a *power* or *will* of his own to *repent* or *believe;* forasmuch as all men are conceived and born in sin, and have inherited from our first parents a corrupt nature, therefore we must submit to the disposal of his sovereign grace, which effectually worketh unto salvation in the elect.

PILGRIM. I do not know that I understand you. Do you mean to say that I can do nothing to get out of this city, and that no man can help me, and yet this city will be destroyed, and all that remain in it? Alas, what shall I do! My poor, poor family!

SOLEFIDIAN. I mean, sir, that I have been within the walls of that gloomy palace long enough to learn that the physicians are very wicked and corrupt, that while they rely upon the virtue of their nostrums they have no virtue in them. It is by *faith alone* you can be saved, and not by works. It is true this city is to be destroyed, and that the original King has provided a city of Refuge for his own sheep, and if you are saved, it will be of his own mercy towards the elect, and if you should be one of the elect you will be saved, being: 1st, Predestinated from all eternity, which is brought; 2d, by *particular redemption* made for the elect, which will be made manifest to you; 3d, by an *irresistable call* which effectually takes away; 4th, your *original sin,* and will result, 5th, in your *final perseverance.* These five points being essential to secure so great a salvation will, in the King's own good time, bring you to a place of safety.

PILGRIM. But, sir, is this copy a correct report of the *ouranographers*, or a partial and corrupt extract? if so, what does it mean where it says, "He tasted death for every man"? (Heb. ii. 9.) And that whosoever will, may go to the city of Refuge (Rev. xxii. 17), and that the King commands all everywhere to do so, (Acts xvii. 30), declaring also that all who do not shall be destroyed? (2 Thes. i. 9.)

SOLEFIDIAN. That, sir, is a correct report, and it contains "all things necessary to life and godliness." (2 Pet. i. 3.) It is so complete that the elect can find enough there for doctrine, reproof, correction and instruction in righteousness. (2 Tim. iv. 16.) But, still, those sayings can only be understood when the King sends a companion of his, called *Paraclete*, whose business it is to open to the eyes of the elect the inner or spiritual meaning. It is true he tasted death for all the elect, and that the reprobate will be destroyed, and the number of each is definitely and unalterably fixed.

PILGRIM. These things being so, probably I may as well wait the King's own good time. In the meantime, I cannot return to my old employers, and so I might as well go and talk to those I see coming yonder.

SOLEFIDIAN. That is a good inclination. It will make the matter no better by going back; but as to these men coming, they may try to console you, but they all agree with me, as the discoverer, that all men that are saved must be saved by *faith alone*.

CHAPTER III.

PILGRIM GOES ON, AND CONVERSES WITH OTHERS—COMES ACROSS MR. EVANGELIST—SEES A LIGHT AHEAD.

Prove all things. Hold fast that which is good.—1 THESS. v. 27.

THE hearing of these things brought Pilgrim into a sad plight, partly on account of not being able to understand it, from not knowing whether the King meant that he should flee for refuge, or whether he would come himself in his own good time and bring him away, or whether, indeed, he was one of those whom the King had decreed to be saved, or to perish with the destruction of the city. Indeed, these thoughts so distracted his mind that he slackened his pace, as he saw some of the men coming toward him; and he sat down on a stone by the wayside, and was wholly absorbed in thought, having the book closed in his hand, when he was startled by a deep, sepulchral groan, and, springing to his feet, he saw before him a queer combination of *candor* and *levity*, humility and pride, authority and submission, of *method* and *disorder*, mounted upon a beast that looked as though it had been rode too much, or had too thin fare.

CIRCUIT RIDER. My dear friend (a groan), you seem to be in trouble. Might I be permitted to inquire as to the cause of your distress?

PILGRIM. Sir, I have learned that this, our city, is to be destroyed by fire, together with all the inhabitants who do not make haste to retire to a place of safety, and I don't know which road to take; and as I ran to make inquiry of my neighbors, some told me one thing, others another. The man whom I have just left yonder says if I am a special favorite with the King of the city of Refuge, he will secure my safety. And yet I feel as though I could not wait. *What shall I do?*

CIRCUIT RIDER, (groaning). Sir, let me warn you against listening to any such men. The Pope, who is very antichrist, did so entirely corrupt religion, that there was nothing left but forms and ceremonies; and that monk, Luther, only broke the hollow shell of *works*, and just discovered the kernel of *faith*, which Calvin, in trying to develop in the darkness around him, concluded that the merit of faith could only accrue to the *elect*, or a few, for whom the Lord died; but let me tell you—blessed be God!—that the Lord died for all. (Amen, shouted a voice behind them, which proved to be a Universalist.) Yes, thank God! he bled and died on Calvary, to reconcile offended deity to man, and his spirit strives with every heart; and, as I see, that spirit is striving with you, I beseech you not to resist it, but go right forward to the *mourning bench*, and we will pray for you. It may be God will be appeased, and will come down and will convert your soul.

PILGRIM, (holding up his book.) Did you ever see this volume of the reports of the *ouranographers?*

I find here an allusion to a city of Refuge, and it says, unless a man be born again, he cannot enter it. (John iii. 3.) Now, sir, I desire to get to a place of safety.

CIRCUIT RIDER. Glory to God! Yes, you must be born again; that is, you must be baptized with the Holy Ghost. You must struggle, and agonize, and hold on. It may be the Lord will turn from his fierce anger, and give you *faith* to *believe* to the saving of your soul. As to that volume, it is nothing but a dead letter that killeth; but when the power comes—bless God!—you can no longer resist, you will experience the joys of the new birth in sins forgiven, and you will know it by your feelings.

PILGRIM. And can it be possible that so great grace is free to all, and that the Lord is willing I should have it? Then what must I do to obtain it?

CIRCUIT RIDER. Most certainly; but, as I told you, you must use the means of grace before mentioned, or I will pray for you here, if you wish; and you must pray, also, powerfully for yourself, for the Lord will be sought unto, that he may do this great thing for you. Like the poor Prodigal, you must come pleading earnestly, and the Holy Ghost has promised to give you repentance unto life.

PILGRIM. But still it seems dark; something seems to say, how shall they call on him in whom they do not believe? If this is the work of the Lord, and the Lord is no respecter of persons, then why should I not wait till the Lord comes this way and converts me?

UNIVERSALIST, (who had been listening near.) Ah, yes! Do you not see the absurdity of all those orthodox notions. The fact is, you have all got only a few faint rays of light from the Infinite Source of love, and these you have perverted, and are comparing the ways of God to your own foolish ways, whereas his ways are not your ways (Isa. lxv. 8), while he is no respecter of persons. He can have compassion on ignorant, and those that are out of the way. He is good alike to all, sending his rain upon the evil and good, and causing his sun to shine upon the just and unjust. And although he permits sin to reign for a little, yet "in the dispensation of the fulness of time he will" save all. As Mr. Monk said, "Christ will save all for whom he died;" and as Mr. Circuit Rider said, "He died for all." Therefore, all will be saved, and this covers the whole ground.

PILGRIM. But, sir, before I saw either of these men, I learned from these reports that our city was to be burned, and with it all who did not obey the gospel. (2 Thess. i. 8.) And now, sir, if there is any danger here, and any chance to get to a place of safety, I don't want to run any risks.

UNIVERSALIST. I tell you, sir, that the idea that the wicked are to be destroyed is a bugbear borrowed from ancient heathen poets, from Milton, and a few other sources. All that is said about Christ's second coming, and the end of the world, and the everlasting destruction of the wicked, had reference to the destruction of Jerusalem. Orthodox priests use it to frighten the weak-minded with. But He that worketh all things after the counsels of his own will, intends to make all happier in heaven than though sin had not existed—as they to whom much is forgiven will love much. (Luke vii. 47.) He will take all alike to his bosom at last, for he is no respecter of persons, and none shall pluck them out of his hands (Isa. vi. 39), but he will raise all up at the last day, and we shall be like the angels, being children of the resurrection.

PILGRIM. But, sir, is this proclamation from the *Great King* (Mark xvi. 16), and if so will it make any difference with us whether we heed it or not? Oh! can it be possible that the end of the world, and the dreadful destruction threatened, the second death, the lake that burneth with fire and brimstone, the quenchless fire, and undying worm, all had allusion to the calamities of Jerusalem? That the penalty of damnation connected with that proclamation, that has caused me so much trouble, did not reach this side of Jerusalem? Alas! this only allays my fears by deepening the gloom that is arising around me.

UNIVERSALIST. True, very true; the darkest hour is just before day. I was rocked in the cradle of orthodoxy, and I know that they see through a glass darkly, because they lean to their own understanding and righteousness, and think to limit the Holy One, by making him partial, and cruel, and changeable. Whereas, God is a God of love, and changes not; therefore, we are not consumed. He says, "Look unto me, ye ends of the earth, and be ye saved, for I am God, and there is none else. (Isa. xlv. 22, 23.) I have sworn by myself—the word has gone out of my mouth, and shall not return unto me void—that unto me every knee shall bow, and every tongue shall swear. Surely shall one say, In the Lord have I righteousness and strength." Thus "declaring the end from the beginning, and from ancient times the things that are not yet done, saying, My counsel shall stand, and I will do all my pleasure." (Isa. xlvi. 10.) And you see it is not His pleasure that any should perish. (2 Pet. iii. 9.) Hence you see if the city is to be destroyed by fire, we have a Saviour who gave himself a ransom for all, to be testified in due time. (1 Tim. ii. 6.) So that we are all safe.

PILGRIM. Well, really it does seem like distrusting the goodness of the great Father, and also the faithfulness of the mighty Saviour, if he is pledged to save to the utmost; but I can't see what use there is of having a Saviour, or a city of Refuge, if all these threatenings were to the Jews, and were executed in the destruction of Jerusalem. It all looks dark, very dark to me, and I guess I may as well give it all up into the hands of the Lord, and go back to work for my poor family. But yonder comes a pretty intelligent-looking man. I wonder if he would give me any comfort, or only make the matter worse?

UNIVERSALIST. That is Mr. Evangelist. I know him. He is a shrewd, intelligent, upright, pious man, far in advance of those other men you conversed with. But still he entertains the horrible idea of an endless hell. He says this city is to be destroyed, and that all who do not submit to a few outward forms and ceremonies, and shed a few outward tears, join the church, etc., will go to hell. But who does not know that if it is on the ground of righteousness we are to be tried, all are in the same condemnation? If all of grace, then all are equally entitled to salvation. As for the idea of a church, it is all calculated to make a cruel distinction among brethren of the same great family, and to foster the feeling that some are greater favorites with Heaven than others. "Have we not all one Father? Hath not one God created us?" (Mal. ii. 10.) But you can talk with him.

PILGRIM. Good evening, Mr. Evangelist, for such, I am informed, is your name. I am in deep distress and perplexity of mind concerning certain things. I have learned about the destruction of our city, and also concerning a city of Refuge, where it is said a poor man can make a better living, and be secure from the impending destruction; but, on inquiry of my neighbors, they have rather perplexed my mind. Some even said they were going there, but did not seem to know whether there was any definite way; others thought there was no danger. Sir, if I could get any clear directions I would be very much obliged.

EVANGELIST. That is my name, sir. Your case is by no means a singular one, and I think, from past experience, I can sympathize with you, having encountered all those neighbors you speak of. What you have heard concerning this city, and the city of Refuge, is all true; and I judge, from the book you have in your hand, you have learned this much from the right source.

PILGRIM. This, sir, is a copy of the reports of the *ouranographers*, which, when I first read, though it filled me with alarm, and set me all to trembling, yet I fancied I almost saw the flames of wrath descending, and also that I could see the city of Refuge, with its gates wide open (Jo. iii. 15), and could hear a voice saying, "Flee for refuge to the city!" (2 Cor. vi. 2.) Yet, being a little confused and uncertain, I thought to inquire of my neighbors, and now, alas! I know not what to do. Now, sir, if you can tell me what to do, I am still disposed to make an effort.

EVANGELIST. That book, sir, is a reliable report. True, there are a few errors, committed by the clerks who translated it for the press. Still, with your present frame of mind, had you been more careful to examine it, and not fallen in with those neighbors, you would, without doubt, have learned the way, for it is described quite plainly. (Isa. xxxv. 81.) You said you almost saw the gate: had you looked a little longer, you would have seen it distinctly. You say you had read four chapters in that book, written by four different men?

PILGRIM. Yes, and they told about the same story, and agreed in their conclusions that I must flee for my life (Jo. xx. 31), that I became so alarmed, I arose and started.

EVANGELIST. Yes, and had you not turned aside to inquire of your neighbors (Gal. i. 16), but read on into the fifth chapter, you would have found very clear directions; for you do not suppose that the King would have given warning of such danger, and done so much to prepare a place of safety, and still have left the way to that place in doubt? Would this have been wise or kind upon his part? You see that wicket gate in those high and massive walls? (Jo. x. 7.) Go knock there, and they will bring you within the walls, into the suburbs of this great city (Jo. x. 9), and you will find a plain path leading directly through the suburbs to the palace of the city of Refuge (Matt. vii. 14), where the Prince in his beauty sits. (Isa. xxxiii. 17.) And on arriving there he will introduce you to his Father, and then you will be safe. (Heb. ii. 13.)

PILGRIM. I confess my error, sir, and feel deeply humbled. What you say seems clear and consistent. I think I see the gate you point to. (Acts viii. 36.) Is that it, a little to the right, with a ray of light streaming through it? How low it is! (Rom. vi. 3, 4.) I shouldn't think one could pass through it standing erect, if he could at all without getting down very low. But pardon me, sir, if I seem to be hesitating. It may be my mind is thrown a little off the balance, or confused by what I have already seen and heard. And I judge from your appearance and discourse that you can bear with me (1 Pet. iii. 8), and perhaps explain my difficulties, if such they really be.

EVANGELIST. I do not profess, sir, to be wise above what is written in those reports. (1 Cor. iv. 6.) But what aid I can give you is at your service, for I was just coming along the way by the Prince's directions (Mark xvi. 15), to render what aid I could to any I might find desirous of being saved. Your impressions with regard to the gate are correct. In digging to find a rock (Matt. xvi. 16) upon which to build this gate, the crystal waters rose to the very arch, yet the golden light permeates its translucent waves, reveals the gate with great distinctness, and now it stands at this dead level, so that the King must come down from his throne, the conqueror from his chariot, and meet the beggar from the dung-hill on a common footing, and they find these waters, which they must enter to pass through the gate, wash out the diamonds from the crown of earthly pride and the laurel wreaths from the warrior's brow, with the same ease it does the filth from the beggar's tattered robes. (Tim. iii. 5.)

PILGRIM. True, sir, I begin to see all this. But you do not come at my difficulty. You speak of instantly entering into a place of refuge (2 Cor. vi. 2), and yet of a long path beset with many dangers before I shall be fully within the city and made entirely secure. (Rev. ii. 10.) These *ouranographers* speak of an attempt on the part of the Prince to establish a place of refuge, and then of his being killed, and finally of his returning with an army (2 Thess. i. 8) and destroying this rebel prince, burning up his city and all his followers, and gathering all who are willing to enlist under his banner into the great city of Refuge. (Matt. xxiv. 3.) Now, sir, this is what confuses me.

EVANGELIST. I think, sir, I see the cause of your difficulty, and it is not very surprising you should fall into such a mistake, because it is true the Prince of Peace did come into this rebellious province for the sake of establishing a place of safety, and offering the *King's pardon* to all who would ground the weapons of their rebellion. (Acts iii. 31.) The rebel prince gathered his forces and set the battle in array, and mistaking the nature of the struggle, supposed he had succeeded in destroying the Prince of Peace, and putting an end to the whole enterprise. (Matt. xxi. 38.) But soon consternation and dismay spread with a report that he had risen from the dead. (Matt. xxviii. 6.) And sure enough, some of his followers who had fled and secreted themselves appeared in public, and gave strength to this report by boldly proclaiming that he was alive, nay, that he had ascended a throne on the other side of that dark river you see over the plains (Acts ii. 30, 34), which divides his real dominion from that rebel province; but that he had established a representative government here, and set up the gates and given the keys to them (Matt. xvi. 19), and that they were now prepared to take all who were willing to enlist, and let them into the first gate. (Acts ii. 38.) And if they would only follow directions, and keep in the path till they came to the river, they should be taken through the second gate, made of pearl, into the palace itself.

PILGRIM. Joy already begins to animate my heart, for while you have been talking I have been reading along (Acts xvii. 11), and I begin to gain my sight, for as I keep my eyes in the direction of the first gate, the light seems to increase, and as it does, this burden on my back still grows blacker and heavier. Oh! that I could be rid of it. But tell me, sir, more about this gate and this temporary government; are the forces which the Prince of Peace has sent sufficient to defend us from our foes while we remain in these suburbs? for the rebel prince will not fail to do his utmost to destroy us if we refuse to serve him. Are the leaders possessed of sufficient wisdom to carry out the good Prince's wishes? and can we take our whole families, little children and all, with us through the gate?

EVANGELIST. Sir, had it not been for that sad mistake of closing the book to consult your neighbors, you might ere this have been within the gate and treading the path rejoicing; but as it is, I am glad to see you anxious to learn more about it. (Matt. vii. 7.) As to the forces, they are amply able to save unto the uttermost (Heb. v. 7) all that will put themselves under their control and protection. As to wisdom, they are not left to their own discretion, but the Prince himself was with them long enough (Acts i. 3) to instruct them in all things pertaining to this government, and he is himself the "wonderful counsellor, the mighty God, the founder of the everlasting age, the Prince of Peace;" added to this, after he crossed the river and ascended the throne, he sent a minister from his presence, called *Paraclete*, whose sagacity was such that he did not vary one word from the Prince's instructions (Jo. xiv. 15), but ever stood by these officers till they had completed all the arrangements marked out, and graded the path (Jo. xiv. 2, 6), hung the gate (Matt. xvi. 19), builded the wall, and established the towers of defence (Gal. i. 8), so that it is dangerous to attempt to get in any other way. (Jo. x. 1.) As to your family and little children, they cannot go through the gate till they are able to walk (Heb. xi. 6) and talk; neither can you carry them through, because the gate, though large enough for the largest person, will only admit one at a time, however small.

PILGRIM. Alas! alas! and must I leave my children, exposed to those dreadful dangers, all alone! I cannot go, if I must leave my dear little ones; would that I had never been born! Can the Prince be good, if he will refuse to let me bring my little ones I love so dearly? If his city is too good for them, it is too good for me! What shall I do? What shall I do?

EVANGELIST. Sir, I supposed, from what you said, you had respect for the good Prince; but you show, by your present emotions, that you have not. (Luke ix. 62.) As to your children, the Prince has made provision for them (Matt. x. 16), and instead of requiring you to desert them and leave them exposed, he holds every parent responsible to take proper care of them (Eph. vi. 4); hence you should examine more closely before you give way to such outbursts of feeling.

PILGRIM. True, sir, I do feel reproved by your just remarks, and confess that I spoke from the impulse of untaught affection. If what you say of the Prince's arrangements be true, I have greatly abused him by indulging for a moment such thoughts. But, sir, I heard my neighbor, Mr. Circuit Rider, say that he had his little ones with him, and declared as warmly as I spoke that if he could not take them along, he wouldn't go himself. If the place of refuge (Rom. xiv. 23) was too good for his children, it was too good for him; and perhaps I got those feelings from him. But, sir, I now see and love the Prince more than ever. Oh! I do believe; help thou mine unbelief. (Mark ix. 24.)

EVANGELIST. If any man lack wisdom, and will only seek in the right direction for it, he shall find. (James i. 5.) If, then, you desire to be better acquainted with the King's plans and arrangements, come with me to this eminence (Rom. xv. 4), and I will show you a model that may aid you in comprehending the whole thing.

CHAPTER IV.

ON ASCENDING THE EMINENCE, EVANGELIST INTRODUCED PILGRIM INTO A LARGE AND SPACIOUS HALL, HUNG ROUND WITH CURIOUS PAINTINGS PREPARED BY THE GREAT KING. HE IS MUCH ENTERTAINED, AND GOES ON HIS WAY REJOICING.

See that thou make all things after the pattern shown to thee in the Mount.—EXOD. xxv. 9.

BOTH being now much interested, and Pilgrim much pleased with anything pertaining to the good Prince and his new government, they arose and ascended the eminence before them slowly, for poor Pilgrim was yet burdened with his black heavy load. But as he saw Mr. Evangelist was anxious to render all the aid in his power to enable him to get rid of it, he went willingly, but as they drew near a stately looking edifice, surrounded with beautiful grounds, he shrank back a little, till reassured of the kindness of the master of the house (Rev. xxii. 17) by Mr. Evangelist. They approached arm in arm, when Mr. Evangelist gave a knock at the door (Acts xvii. 3), and soon the door was opened by a very polite, cheerful porter, who pleasantly asked them what they desired; when Mr. Evangelist said he had brought a friend, who was desirous to learn more concerning Prince Immanuel's land and kingdom, and if his master, Mr. Interpreter, would be pleased to show him through the hall, he would take it as a favor, for the more he talked with his neighbors the more confused his mind became.

At this, the porter, with a hearty good will, conducted them to his master, who received them courteously, and perceiving that they were somewhat weary, ordered food and drink to be set before them (1 Pet. ii. 2), of which poor Pilgrim ate and drank with a pleasure he had never experienced before, and turning to Evangelist said, What can make this food so delicious, seeing it has none of that seasoning my neighbors use so lavishly, in order to make their entertainments palatable? To which Evangelist replied, the good Prince prepared it himself (Job xvi. 13), and he knew just what was most appropriate to restore our tastes, and then what was best for us to eat. (Job ii. 25.)

So when they had refreshed themselves, Mr. Interpreter took them into a large picture gallery, hung with splendid paintings, which at first seemed a little dim from age. (1 Cor. x. 11.) But when their eyes were a little more used to the light they saw clearer, and were much pleased with the beautiful and majestic order that seemed to prevail.

Poor Pilgrim especially seemed filled with wonder and delight, and turning to the right, before they advanced, his attention was directed by Mr. Interpreter to a very curious picture (Gal. iv. 24), which he said was painted as a sort of frontispiece by a very skillful and erudite artist, who had studied in the best schools in the world. (Acts xxii. 3.) In fact, it was a sort of key or bird's eye view of all the pictures in the hall.

PILGRIM. May I be permitted to ask who that female is standing near that burning, dreadful mountain, with fetters on her hands—what does it mean?

INTERPRETER. That, sir, is Hagar, the bondmaid of an ancient patriarch called Abraham, and signifies that all his merely fleshy descendants were to be in bondage, or under the law of Moses, which would not let them be free. (Acts xv. 10.)

PILGRIM. But that smiling old lady and little boy, on the other end of the canvass, who are they?

INTERPRETER. That is Sarah, the lawful wife of the old patriarch, and a son of her's born out of his natural time. These signify the place of Refuge, of which Brother Evangelist has no doubt spoke.

EVANGELIST. Permit me to say that this picture will appear plainer to Mr. Pilgrim after he sees the rest, for then he will see it is all an attempt to prepare the mind, and point out the way to the city of Refuge. (Isa. xl. 3; lvii. 14.)

INTERPRETER. True, Brother Evangelist, but you must not hurry our friend Pilgrim, for I perceive he not only has a heavy burden to carry, but by reason of the distraction of his mind (Matt. xxiv. 24), the film before his eyes (Col. ii. 22), he moves cautiously and sees indistinctly.

Whereupon, taking Pilgrim gently by the hand he led him along a little further, and showed him another large, beautiful painting, in a gilt frame, before which Pilgrim stood wrapt in a sort of dreamy mood, while

Mr. Interpreter took from his hand the volume of Reports he still held, and turning a few leaves read (Acts vii.) a description of it, saying—

INTERPRETER. This is a sort of masterpiece, drawn by one of the *ouranographers* named Stephen. It was intended to show that, after many and long preparations, the Prince of Peace had come, and that able prime minister, Prince Paraclete, was now directing his affairs, whose servants it was as dangerous to resist as the great Prince himself. (Matt. x. 40.)

PILGRIM. Do I understand you, that this minister Paraclete was sent as soon as the Prince took his seat on his throne, and that he has been present in these suburbs ever since?

INTERPRETER. Yes, sir; he always stands by every soldier of the Prince when in full armor (Jo. xiv. 16), and wherever their sword (Eph. vi. 17), the old Jerusalem blade, makes a mortal wound, or so pierces the heart of an enemy as to slay him, he puts forth his hand and raises them up, and breathes into them new life. (Gal. iv. 6.)

PILGRIM. This seems to me strange and wonderful. But pray what does this next picture mean? It looks like a tabernacle surrounded by a vast multitude of people, and those who are serving around it seem to have veils on.

That, sir, is a piece by Moses, the great law-giver of the Jews, and is very instructive indeed. He attempted a picture of the city of Destruction, and the suburbs of the city of Refuge, but because of the obstinacy of the people in failing to see the path he had thus marked out, they are represented with veils over their faces. (2 Cor. iii. 13–16.)

At this explanation Pilgrim felt a little amused, but was soon brought to a very sober frame of mind, as Interpreter turning to him said, "Beware lest ye also fail after the same manner of unbelief." (Heb. iv. 14.) Whereat Pilgrim trembled, and said the whole thing began to be so interesting and plain he knew not at what he smiled, the pleasure he experienced or the folly of the Jews. Both felt a stronger desire than ever to know more.

Does this multitude represent the world in rebellion and the Tabernacle the city of Refuge?

INTERPRETER. It may be looked upon in that light. For on passing through this opening in the string of curtains that surrounds the real Tabernacle, called the outer court, you see first he has painted a large altar (Ex. xl. 6); a little further on, in a direct line to the door of the Tabernacle, stands a large laver (Ex. xl. 7, 30, 32) for bathing. You remember a little wicket gate, Brother Evangelist, pointed out to you in the walls of the city—well, this bath represents that (Tim. iii. 5), for all must be washed before they enter the sanctuary, as it is called, or the first room in the Tabernacle (Is. iii. 5), and which represents the suburbs of the great city of Refuge.

PILGRIM. But, sir, did all the multitude bathe and then enter in here, to this sanctuary?

INTERPRETER. No, sir. Only the tribe called the priests.

PILGRIM. The reason of my asking the question

4

was, I heard neighbor Circuit Rider say that circumcision was the door into the Jewish church; but at the time, not caring much for these things, I noticed but little what he said.

INTERPRETER. No, they were *born* members of the Jewish church; but this picture was especially designed to illustrate the city of Refuge, with the manner of getting into it, and the employment of its inhabitants. Probably Mr. Circuit Rider said but little about this picture, because it had no mourning bench, although the *ouranographers* called special attention to it (Heb. 9), as a beautiful representation of the city of Refuge. And the fact that none but priests went in here is also suggestive, since all that get into these suburbs are priests (1 Pet. ii. 9); and it may also aid us in understanding why little children are not taken in, since they cannot become priests.

PILGRIM. But Mr. Evangelist told me there was ample provision made for their protection by the good Prince, who had a special care for them.

INTERPRETER. Yes. Those walls and battlements, if the priests are faithful, will be crowded with unslumbering soldiers, supplied with abundant ammunition, so that no harm need befall them. (1 Pet. v. 8.)

PILGRIM. But I notice within that little enclosure he has painted a table, with what seems to be twelve loaves of bread on it, a beautiful little altar, and a curious candlestick. What of these?

INTERPRETER. Well, these are all to represent certain things you will find in the suburbs, called the Lord's table, altar of prayer, and the words of the great Prince, which seem to shed light upon the duty of all the priests, like lamps. (Jo. viii. 12.) There are also many other interesting and useful points about this painting.

PILGRIM. But what does *that* picture represent?

INTERPRETER. That, sir, was drawn by the celebrated painter, *John*, representing a scene that produced an immense excitement in the land of Judæa, just before the good Prince came. That eccentric looking personage in the centre, standing in the water, with majestic bearing, is called *Forerunner*, because he came to introduce the Prince (Jo. i. 7) to the rebels.

PILGRIM. Truly, he has drawn a great crowd around him; and they seem strangely agitated. But there is another picture, a little to the left, that fills me with peculiar feelings. It is similar to this, but it seems to be a city filled with a dense crowd, in a state of still greater alarm, looking with pale and haggard faces toward the heavens, and what strikes me with peculiar force, is, they seem to have upon their backs, burdens similar to mine. (Acts ii. 37.)

INTERPRETER. Truly, sir, you have now come to an interesting picture, the master-piece of the beloved physician, Luke, whose profound learning rather qualified him to paint to the life. These rebels, as Brother Evangelist no doubt told you, put the good Prince to death, and supposed they had destroyed him, for they had said, "let his blood be upon us and on our children." (Matt. xxvii. 25.) But what was their surprise to learn a few mornings after, that he had not only risen from the dead but crossed beyond the river, and established his throne where they could not reach him, and that he had collected forces enough to crush the whole of them. (Acts ii. 35.) And this so alarmed them, that expecting every day to be crushed, they heard a sound as of a rushing mighty wind (Acts ii. 2), in the direction of the Prince's dominions, and looking up as you see in the picture, it proved to be the chariot of his prime minister, Prince Paraclete, who came with all the celestial pomp of state, and driving in his chariot at once to the legislative hall, where his senators were assembled (Acts ii. 3), he delivered the good Prince's message (Acts ii. 3), to the twelve whom he had chosen, to be his special ministers; and instantly placed upon the head of each a crown, that seemed like brilliant flames. And rising to their feet (14 *v.*) with most unaccountable dignity and composure, (for they had fled away from the people for fear of their lives), they began to address the multitude who had crowded into the hall, still railing and mocking. (13 *v.*)

Pilgrim. Truly that was an exciting occasion, and the recital of it gives me very strange feelings. But who is that bold looking fellow in the front, with his hand stretched out, as though he was addressing the people, with such unearthly earnestness expressed in his countenance?

Interpreter. That is one of the twelve prime ministers, named Peter. The artist has seized the moment to draw when Peter was addressing the excited populace. And he had no sooner began to speak than a solemn feeling, such as they had never known before, spread itself over the vast assembly, when he went on to rehearse the history of the good Prince, while he was among them (Acts ii. 22) up to the time they had so wickedly killed him; and then declared that he had been raised up from the dead, as they already knew. That he had established his throne on the other side of the river, and collected forces enough to crush all his foes. But that he had now directed them to say to all the rebels who would lay down their arms, and join under his banner, that they should be pardoned. (38 *v.*) When he came to this point the anxiety of the multitude was such that they gave one wild shriek, and said, "What shall we do?" (37 *v.*)

PILGRIM. Oh! sir, I don't know why it is, but I seem to have some of their feelings, although I was not present to stain my hands in his blood, yet this burden presses upon my heart some, as that blood did upon them. And I have a strange feeling that if I cannot get rid of it, my fate must be as bad as theirs. Certainly, sir, I feel that I stand in the same relation to the good Prince that they did.

INTERPRETER. If this picture helps to make you feel so, then the painter is but successful, for that was his object, and this was the reason why it was hung in this hall. (1 Cor. ii. 2.) And, sir, unless you learn the lesson of this painting, and improve upon it, you cannot escape the fate of the city of Destruction.

PILGRIM. But, sir, there is one more painting that sets me to trembling, what can it mean? There seems to be a still greater crowd assembled than in any of the others. But they seem to be divided into two assemblies. And there seems to be a third group, partly between, and above them in the air, as it were. And all the colors are far deeper, more brilliant and terrible, than any of the other pictures.

INTERPRETER. You did well that you caught a sight of that canvass. It is the master-piece of the whole hall, and one of so dreadful a description, and whose terrible impression it was expected would be so deep, and ought to be so truthful, that the good Prince drew it himself (Matt. xxiv. 30), as descriptive of his second coming to this rebellious province, when he intends to bring every one that lives here, or ever has lived, up before him (2 Cor. v. 10), and then he will separate all whose burdens have been removed, into a company by themselves, as you see on the right hand; and all that have burdens like that upon your back, into another, as you see, on his left. That is the good Prince himself you see elevated in front, and those are angels standing around him, on poised wing, ready, when he gives command, to drag all that persist in their rebellion out, and cast them into a lake burning with fire and brimstone (Rev. xix. 20), from whence the smoke of their torment will ascend for ever and ever. And ready also to escort all who lay down their arms and accept of his favor, up to that gate you see away beyond him out of which flows such a soft, beautiful light, into the *real city* of everlasting refuge (Rev. xxii. 14), where they will be safe for ever. May the good Prince have mercy on us all.

As he said this they were standing near the door; and Mr. Evangelist, seeing poor Pilgrim tremble so that he could scarcely keep his feet, took him by the arm, and they passed out of the hall and walked slowly on for some little distance before either could recover himself enough to speak, when Pilgrim, as though suddenly coming to himself, started up, exclaiming: This scene has filled my mind with new and strange emotions, and yet there is one point about which I want a little more information. When those rebels cried out, as Mr. Interpreter said, to know what they should do, I desire to know if Peter informed them? for it seems to me what was necessary in their case is also in mine, for I cannot get rid of the impression that all these things meant me!

EVANGELIST. Truly, sir. Peter told them most pointedly what they should do; and if it does not all mean you, as you say, you may use it all to your everlasting benefit. He said that they must refuse to bear burdens any longer for the rebels (at this Pilgrim's eyes brightened, for he had done this), or repent, and that they must be baptized (Acts ii. 38), or pass through the little gate I showed you, and pledge themselves to bear burdens (Luke xiv. 27) for the good Prince, which are light and pleasing. (Matt. xi. 30.) And as he said this, they drew near the little gate they had just descried on entering the Interpreter's hall, when Pilgrim said, with much earnestness, What hinders me from being baptized? (Acts viii. 36.) If this is the way I am to get rid of this burden, let us not delay.

EVANGELIST. If you believe with all your heart, you may.

PILGRIM. I do believe with all my heart that Jesus, the good Prince, came down from heaven; that he was anointed of God with power to save to the uttermost; and above all things, I do desire to be rid of this burden, and am willing to go into the floods or flames, if that is what he wants.

So, pausing beside a beautiful stream that meanders close by the walls of the suburbs, they both went down into the water, and Evangelist baptized him, "into the name of the Father, Son, and Holy Spirit." And coming up out of the water, Pilgrim not only found his burden gone, but felt such a strong joy at his heart, and so light ot frame, that he could have leaped like a roe; neither could he refrain from singing (joined by Evangelist)—

'Tis done, the great transaction's done
  I am the Lord's, and he is mine;
He drew me, and I followed on,
  Rejoiced to own the call divine.

Now rest, my long divided heart,
  Fixed on this blissful centre, rest;
Here have I found a nobler part;
  Here heavenly pleasures fill my breast.

High Heaven that hears the solemn vow,
   That vow renewed shall daily hear
Till in life's latest hour I bow,
   And bless in death a bond so dear.

CHAPTER V.

HAVING THUS FOUND THE GATE OPENING INTO THE KING'S HIGHWAY, PILGRIM IS STILL ENTRANCED WITH THE CLEAR, SOFT LIGHT THAT GRADUALLY BREAKS AROUND HIM—AND STILL GOES ON REJOICING—BUT SOON COMES TO THE HILL DIFFICULTY—FINALLY ARRIVES AT THE CITY OF ORTHODOXY.

Therefore we are buried with him by baptism into death, that like as Christ was raised up by the glory of the Father, even so we also should walk in newness of life.—ROM. vi. 4.

WHEN Pilgrim had thus given vent to his feelings, Evangelist turns to him with a benevolent and affectionate countenance, and taking him by the hand, says:

EVANGELIST. My dear brother, all you read in that blessed volume of the *ouranographers*, concerning your danger and the fate of your native city is still true, and from your situation you are still exposed to the smoke and flames, which may set your own dwelling on fire (1 Cor. ix. 27), and I would, therefore, advise you to be on your watch (Mar. xiii. 34), and never idle. (Phil. ii. 12.) Remember the picture gallery and the instructions given to you by the interpreter. You have, as you see, just entered the wicket gate, opening through the walls of the city of Destruction (Col. i. 13) into the suburbs of the city of Refuge; but you should not feel that all is done. This book I am still glad to see in your hand, written by those *ouranographers*, shows much candor, and wisdom, and earnestness, inasmuch as they saw the danger (2 Cor. v. 11), they were anxious to rouse the inhabitants to a sense of their danger, and then show them clearly how they might get to a place of perfect and everlasting safety. (1 Tim. iii. 15.) And you will also notice the book is arranged with much taste and skill, and it is divided into distinct subjects, so that there need be no difficulty after all in understanding all that is important.

Four of these men, who were looking at the heavens (Acts xxvi. 7) with great earnestness, happened to stand where they could see clearly (Acts i. 21), wrote out their observations and convictions that the city would be destroyed, and at the same time discovered a clue to the way of escape. (John xx. 31.) This part of the book, it appears, you had read when, in the midst of the alarm, naturally enough produced thereby, you ran to consult your neighbors. But you see that the second chapter, written by one of them who was exactly qualified for the task, sets forth, without a single *figure* or dark saying, the manner in which they themselves directed individuals out of the city of Destruction (Acts ii. 38, 47) into the suburbs of the city of Refuge; neither did they stop here, but, knowing full well that the journey might be hazardous and long, they went further, and added another chapter, containing some *twenty-one* paragraphs or letters, to show all such as were disposed to start how they might reach the gate of the *great city* and enter and be forever safe. (2 Pet. i. 5.) Now I hope you will study this *third* chapter attentively, and, as you value life and everything that is dear, see that you follow the directions given there, and don't go to your neighbors to inquire the way.

PILGRIM. My dear sir, you bring strange things to my ears, and I do feel still reproved for shutting up this blessed book that alone gave me a knowledge of these things, and that I am satisfied alone could give me directions to escape, and going in my alarm and haste, to inquire of my neighbors; and, what is a little remarkable, the *mist* or *fog* that seemed to obscure everything or blind my eyes begins to pass away, and the light grows clearer and clearer. Blessed be Immanuel that I was not left a prey to that distracted state of mind I felt when listening to my neighbors.

"This is the way I long have sought,
And mourned because I found it not;
My grief a burden long had been,
Because I was not saved from sin."

And suiting the action to the words, Pilgrim set forward with much vigor, accompanied by Evangelist, insomuch that they soon began to pant for breath, and began to weary a little, when they saw a beautiful arbor (Heb. x. 25), whereinto they turned aside and sat down to rest themselves and talk a little further.

EVANGELIST. Be of good cheer, my brother, although this path may at times be rough and steep, and even thorny, yet you will find these sweet resting places all along, provided with many refreshments, and what is more there are beautiful little observatories built on them by directions of Immanuel himself (Matt. xxviii. 20); from which if you will always look (2 Pet. i. 9; Heb. ii. 1), you will obtain the assurance that an anxious pilgrim knows how to appreciate, that you are in the way that will, in the end, bring you to the city. (1 John v. 4.)

PILGRIM. True, sir, I feel a little fatigued but not at all discouraged, but even if I did, your words seem to fill my soul with hope and courage, and even a curious anxiety (2 Pet. iii. 18), to ascend one of these observatories and take a still further view of the road.

EVANGELIST. This, my dear brother, is a good indication, and if you will only follow this inclination which leads you to examine the road and surrounding country from these observatories (2 Tim. iii. 16), you will be safe.

PILGRIM. (Taking the telescope which Evangelist held in his hand, and putting it to his eye.) Oh, how beautiful and plain. It looks like a highway instead of an obscure one. True, it seems narrow, but so straight and plain. I wonder that any should miss it. And there seems to be guide-boards placed at convenient distances, and plainly inscribed.

There is one on the right hand side which says, "Refuse profane and old wives' fables, and exercise thyself unto godliness." (1 Thess. iv. 7.) And another one still which says, "He hath given us all things which pertain to life and godliness through the knowledge of Him that hath called us to glory and virtue." (2 Pet. i. 3.) And still another, which reads, "Run with patience the race that is set before you, looking unto Jesus the author and finisher of the faith." (Heb. xii. 1.) Truly, these inscriptions seem like an unseen hand grasping my soul and impelling me on in this direction.

EVANGELIST. Thus, you see, the gracious Prince has been at great pains to set up these guide boards, having had the whole ground surveyed and graded, and under the superintendence of that skilful engineer Paraclete. These inscriptions were painted and put up for the benefit of pilgrims (1 Tim. iii. 16), and if you will only follow their directions you will arrive in the city of Refuge, although on the way you may find trials, perhaps some bad roads, occasionly a little hill, pass through some villages and cities, meet with many that will question you, and try to lead you astray. But watch thou in all things, give good heed to these inscriptions and all will be well.

And so taking an affectionate leave of him, Evangelist departed and left Pilgrim to pursue his way, which he did with a joyful heart, wondering in himself at all these things. And now he found what he had not expected; and that was, that his trembling and anxiety had given place to great peace and joy, in believing. (Rom. xv. 13.) Suddenly a light shone round him, and gazing around in surprise at its strangely soft, silvery, and confronting radiance, he saw that it proceeded from that heavenly messenger, Paraclete, that stood fast by the little gate where he had just entered, who now approached smilingly and offered to accompany him (Acts ii.), at the same time sealing the King's name in his forehead and giving him a white stone with a new name in it (Rev. ii. 17); then prostrating himself, he poured from a warm and grateful heart a prayer of thanksgiving and praise. Then, arising, he sang the beautiful song ending,

"Since from His bounty I receive
Such proofs of love divine,
Had I a thousand hearts to give
Lord, they should all be thine."

As they journeyed on, Pilgrim's joy was great to find this light increased, but he had not gone far before he came to a little village situated on the left side of the road called *Worldlymindedness*, inhabited by the descendants of *Ease, Avarice, Self-conceit and Sceptic.* The old folks had died of various diseases induced by their mode of living, while some had been hanged for their crimes, others died in prison, yet a large posterity still remained.

While Pilgrim passed along the streets and saw the manner in which they spent their lives, his spirit was stirred within him, and he thought he could easily convince them of the error of their ways, for he was not one to keep still after what he had learned and now enjoyed. So, thinking they would all understand him, he raised his voice, exclaiming, "Ho! every one that thirsteth, come ye to the waters, come and buy wine and milk without money and without price." Whereat some stopped their sports, others their sweating labors, or counting of gold, and gathered around, thinking here was some new adventure for pleasure or profit. When Pilgrim, perceiving that he was misapprehended, began to reprove them for their sins, and told them that their village was to be burned with fire, and they too, unless they repented. Whereupon Mr. Sceptic, seeing the sons of Ease and Avarice showing signs of fear, replied with a confident tone, "All things seemed to be as calm as they were from the beginning of the world, I see no signs of danger." But Ease, wishing to give some apology, said, "All stand in need of a little recreation, and we do but engage in innocent sports, and while away our time with the news and tobacco, and a little social conviviality.

PILGRIM. A good man advises, "To read our Bibles to be gay," and you had better spend your time in that kind of recreation that will not end in sorrow.

SELF-CONCEIT. I take it that a man's conscience is the best guide. We try to do about what is right, and I guess no great harm will come of *that*. We mind our own business. And reason teaches me that there is nothing better than to eat and drink and be merry, and enjoy the good of our labor.

PILGRIM. It is certainly comfortable to have a good estimate of ourselves; but I have been reading in this book that the city of Destruction and all these villages are to be burned up—that unless you flee to a place of safety, your joy will be turned to mourning.

SCEPTIC. I perceive you are troubled about what that book says. You are not the first one who has been perplexed about it. I wish it were burned, and men left to the light of nature. Then should the unfettered mind soar aloft, and bask in the clear sunshine of pure induction, and nature open its wonderful *arcana* to teach man wisdom.

How far this discussion would have gone, is uncertain, had not a *Mr. Wanton,* a crafty fellow of the baser sort, gathered together a company of gay, careless daughters of the village, and brought them, half naked and dancing, in a wanton manner before the crowd; whereupon Pilgrim, remembering the warnings of Evangelist, hastened into the road, wondering at the profaneness and ignorance of the people, and their hardness of heart, seeming to be united in deceiving each other. But he afterwards heard that his brief visit and plain appeal had taken root. Many of their sports ceased, and many became more thoughtful.

Pilgrim had not gone far from the village before he came to the foot of a hill called *Difficulty*. Now, being a little alarmed at the prospect before him, and wearied by his recent encounter, he turned aside to refresh himself at a beautiful spring. (Rev. xxi. 6.) Here he found one of his fellow-townsmen, *Fidelity*, for whose company he was very glad just now, as he felt the need of some firm and prudent companion.

They had scarcely embraced, with joyful and mutual surprise, and taken a cooling drink of the sweet spring, when they saw one running toward them, along a road on the right side of the hill. His clothes were dusty and disordered, his countenance pale and dejected, and he trembled exceedingly. Taking no notice of the pilgrims, he turned, and began to ascend the hill as fast as he could. Seeing which, Fidelity called out, "Ho! friend, have you not a mind to keep us company."

SINCERITY. I have for some time been anxiously seeking the way from the city of Destruction to the city of Refuge, and have been so often directed to the right, and then to the left, and so deceived by company, that I am afraid of every man I meet, and have concluded I can get on as well alone as in company.

FIDELITY. True; there are so many lo! here's, and lo! there's, that one is liable to be distracted, and needs to be a little choice in selecting company. Still, we need company, and should hold fast that which is good. The hill before us, as you see, is very rugged, and as it lays in our path, we ought to get all the aid we can to ascend it.

Sincerity then came, hesitatingly, and drank of the spring, for he was very thirsty, and then together they betook themselves to ascend the hill, singing,

> Together let us sweetly live,
>   Together let us die,
> And each a starry crown receive,
>   And reign in worlds on high."

Notwithstanding they felt refreshed and vigorous at the outset, yet they soon began to pant for breath, because the hill was steep, when suddenly they came to a little arbor, where they sat down to rest and talk a little; and, by request, Sincerity related a little of his experience, saying, I was born in the city of Destruction. My father's name was *Orthodox.* I was, from a child, inclined to be thoughtful, and while searching for books to gratify my thirst for reading, I found in an obscure part of the house a copy of the *Reports,* such as I see Brother Pilgrim have. The entire connection of my father's family claimed to have this book, and to use it as their guide, but the more I read it the more I was troubled to reconcile their practices with what the *book* said. One day the minister of our parish visited our house, to whom my father told my difficulty; when he undertook to explain how all the different members of the Orthodox family, which were very numerous and respectable, agreed in the main, though they differed in some minor matters. That if the heart was only right, it did not matter *what* we believed, for all were agreed that we were justified by *faith only;* that if I had only faith to believe, the good Prince would grant repentance unto life. I asked him about the reports. He said it was, without doubt, all true, but that it was a dead letter, and of no use till Paraclete came to our aid, and that he would enlighten and guide us in the right way. But on inquiring of him as to the right way, he was very indefinite, and finally said it did not make much difference what way I took so I got there. It would never be asked what way I came. Not being satisfied with the indefinite answer, I resolved to start, which I did with emotions faintly exhibited by my appearance when you first saw me. Resolving to keep aloof from all company, vaguely thinking I could get to the city of Refuge as well "out of the church as in it." But now I feel glad that you induced me to join your company. It is, indeed, good for me to be here. These lines now express my feelings:

"I love thy kingdom, Lord,
The house of thine abode;
The church our blest Redeemer bought
With his own precious blood."

PILGRIM. Brother, I am glad to hear these things. We should not throw away even a little good because there is so much that is bad.

FIDELITY. It appears to me this hill now we are so near its top, does not seem so steep and *difficult* as when we were at its foot, so let us press on to the top. It is right that it should be high, so that that beautiful city we read of in the Reports should be seen further, as a beacon to those who wish to flee to the city of Refuge.

PILGRIM. I remember Mr. Evangelist said our road lay through a city, and there it is on the top of this hill.

SINCERITY. Pause, my brethren; I trust you will bear with me. I frankly confess my misgivings. But I recognize this as the city of *Orthodoxy*, to which I was taken when I was a babe, and which I visited as I grew up, with different *branches* of my father's family, and found it built with different *streets*. Each one seemed to have its own regulations, and but little intercourse, and where many have been lost.

FIDELITY. True, true. Suppose, however, we spend a few days here making inquiry.

CHAPTER VI.

THE PILGRIMS STOP TO MAKE INQUIRIES, AND ARE SHOWN BY MR. CLERICUS THROUGH THE CITY—FINALLY GET A GLIMPSE OF THE HOUSE BEAUTIFUL.

While one says, I am of Paul, and I of Apollos, and I of Cephas, and I of Christ.—1 COR. i. 12.

THUS conversing, they drew near to the ctiy, and passed quietly along the streets till they came near the centre. And although they found the city very populous, each one wearing a stiff, anxious look, smiling only at those from their own *street*, the pilgrims were but little noticed, till at length they saw a man of more pleasing aspect standing in the door of a corner house, who kept his eye on them till they came up, when he saluted them, and invited them to come in, saying, as he did so, that he took them to be pilgrims. They replied that they were, and were anxious to obtain what information they could. He desired them to be seated, and, after some refreshments, he would give them what information he was able. While supper was being made ready, Sincerity, whose mind had been truly awakened, and his heart filled with a desire to know (James i. 5), and being naturally of an inquisitive turn, said, with much modesty, may I be permitted to inquire by whom we are thus unexpectedly and pleasantly entertained?

CLERICUS. My name is *Clericus*, my father's name was *Episcopas*, who was a worthy son of *Pope Petros*. My grandfather built a large city on the plains of *worldly ambition*, having for its capital a splendid palace, standing on seven hills (Rev. xvii. 3), near the centre of the plain.

PILGRIM. I wonder if that was not it which I saw just on leaving the city of Destruction over to the left hand, surrounded by gloomy walls, whence issued groans and shrieks of helpless females and the blood of innocents, to which Mr. Priest would have sent me?

CLERICUS. The same; and the noise and disorder and outward show of the city grew so apace, and forms and ceremonies so multiplied, notwithstanding the piety of the people had all died out, that my father removed and built this city, but now only occupies one small street, as you shall see, while I, still not thinking my parents had removed quite far enough from the old city, and still retained too many of her ways, left home and built here on the corner of *Church street*, from whence, as you will see, I have pleasant access to the King's highway, and all the other streets of the city; and seeing there is such an inclination to improve the city, and still add new streets and avenues and lanes, I am now watchful, looking around, and endeavoring to cultivate and promote a spirit of friendship between the different wards, and have already called several *world's conventions*, to see what could be done towards maintaining friendly relations and framing a treaty of peace.

SINCERITY. My father lived in this city, and I was born in one of its streets; and I remember, when a boy, of going to meeting in the different streets, and found that the people in each one thought no one could get to the *Celestial city* without going through their street.

CLERICUS. True, I have been much grieved with this spirit, for I think there are good *Christians* living on all these streets. It was on account of this feeling I could not remain at home. Those that lived on my father's street felt and acted as though nobody else could get to heaven but through their street. This opinion they entertained because it fed their bigotry, indulged their idleness, and acted as a sort of salvo to their consciences, making them feel, in process of time, that devotion to their church supplied the lack of piety, that clerical dignity and titles would secure them the homage of the world, and that the orthodoxy of their creed would take them to heaven any way. As to *what* they believed, this was not of account, provided the church was the most *orthodox;* that would keep its doctrine pure. And much of their spirit has been carried to all these streets. Hence, feeling my spirits stirred within me, I have set myself to the business I told you.

Supper being announced, they sat down, when their host *said grace,* after which they did ample justice to the simple repast; after which they sat to converse a little, as they found their host a kind-hearted, intelligent, and communicative man, and, ere they were aware the curtains of evening drew around them, and they were cordially invited to tarry all night, to which they readily consented, as they desired daylight in which to view the city.

As Clericus saw that his guests were weary, he rang a bell, when his family all entered the room, and he proceeded, with the precision of early habit, to read a portion of Scripture, explaining it, and then line a hymn, which all joined to sing; after which they all kneeled down, and Clericus uttered a fervent prayer to the King for a blessing on his guests and family. After this they retired to rest. In the morning, in like manner, did Clericus bless the King for the preservations of the night, and ask for guidance through the day.

While at breakfast, Faithful remarked, "What a happy sight it is to see a family thus ordered and strict in worship!"

CLERICUS. Yes, religion cannot be enjoyed or maintained without it. But, alas! family religion is shamefully neglected throughout our city; and, for this cause, many are weak and sickly among us, and many die. Some make excuses that they are not able to pray, or have not time, or some other equally frivolous ones, which they would be ashamed to make in their worldly business, and, as a result, religion is declining and dying out.

Being thus refreshed, Clericus took his guests out to see the city. He first showed them the walls and gates of the city, which were old and well constructed, but stood much in need of repair. And Clericus said a shrewd man had recently been along examining them, and expressed his conviction that they would not bear repairing, and even proposed to remove them altogether. He was said to have been born in *Scotch* street; then went to *Presbyterian* street, finding the walls there too unsafe, went to *Baptist* street. This he found too straight and narrow; and then went on to the house *Beautiful*, where you may find him, and hear more of his daring plans, for he even proposed to destroy the *By-Laws*, and having nothing but the *Reports* of the *ouranographers* to govern the city by, and direct pilgrims with. He even said that creeds were the *idols* of these different streets, and *bones of contention*, and many other hard things. Although when a noted *giant* came along, and defied the armies of *Orthodoxy* to meet him and defend their religion, this man stood up alone, and won the admiration of the whole city by demolishing the *giant* single-handed. I must confess I loved him for that; and when he again stood up, and, with the greatest champion from Presbyterian street, showed that creeds were unnecessary and injurious, and that the Bible was an all-sufficient rule of faith and practice, I was filled with admiration, and felt almost converted to his plan of throwing away everything but just what the Bible said, and doing just what it bid. But then my scheme of forming a grand Christian Alliance could not be given up, so I had to let him go. I believe that there is some good in every creed, and hence I want to collect this up from all these, and form a sort of general platform for an Evangelical Alliance between all these streets. But this man said it would only form another street, all of which was against the original wish of the *Good Prince*, and must partake more or less of the spirit of rebellion, or, what is as bad, an impeachment of the wisdom of the Prince, virtually charging that his laws are not sufficient for the government of his kingdom, or that they are not sufficiently plain, and hence that these are attempts to supply what is lacking. But I think they pay great respect to the Bible, inasmuch as they all admit the Bible to be an all-sufficient rule of faith and practice, and that what cannot be found written therein or proved thereby is not to be required of any.

SINCERITY. Well, if what you say be true. I think, *Mr. Restorer*—for such I think you call him—has pretty good ground to go upon, and that he is certainly safe in adopting the Bible alone as his standard; and if these streets rather multiply, notwithstanding all your efforts, and new creeds have to be made, I should think you would be for adopting his plan, as you admit all he wants is to see *Christianity restored.*

FAITHFUL. I, for one, feel anxious to see the city, and then go on to the house *Beautiful* and learn more of this *Mr. Restorer.* I think all good pilgrims should be one; and if all the efforts of man at making platforms for the union of Christians only result in making sects, it occurs to me his plan is a good one.

PILGRIM. So many streets leading out of the city of Destruction makes it dangerous for those wishing to escape. It had well nigh proved my destruction, for I became so confused when I started on my pilgrimage I was about to give up in despair, return, and perish with the city; and if there is, as you say, one *straight and narrow way* leading to the city of Refuge, why have they builded on so many streets here?

CLERICUS. Oh, the reason for this would be lengthy. We are now in *Episcopalian street.* You notice this street is kept very clean, and adorned with many very princely buildings. But it has been the scene of fierce, and some bloody, struggles. It is claimed that this street was laid out by a pilgrim by the name of Paul, who was said to have preached in it after he had been imprisoned in the gloomy city you saw on the hills, but was again caught, taken back there, and had his head cut off by one of the wicked rulers of that city. Various mobs arose in this street till about the close of the fifth century. The *Pope* sent emissaries, who succeeded in establishing the Catholic religion, with all its ceremonies.

Thus things continued till the great *Reformation* under Luther, in the fore-part of the 16th century—when Henry VIII., though married to Catharine of Arragon, his brother's widow, yet fell in love with Anne Boleyn. And, because the Pope would not sanction his marrying her, Henry threw off his yoke, and again built up this street.

You see *thirty-nine* beautiful palaces along here; these were built, for the entertainment of all pilgrims who choose to stop in this street, by Edward VI., son of Henry. But in a few months his sister Mary got the power, and again called back the Catholics. In about five years she died, and her half-sister, Elizabeth, got the power, drove off the Catholics, cleaned the palaces, and opened them anew for pilgrims. Mobs troubled the streets, however, till 1660, when Charles II. restored it again.

SINCERITY. Is it not surprising that men should struggle so hard for the mere *non-essentials* or *additions* to religion.

CLERICUS. Yes, I have been laboring to convince the citizens that it is all foolish and wrong. And I think the struggles in this street show that piety and purity do not necessarily go with the claim of priority and infallibility. James II., brother of Charles, came near restoring the Catholic rule. But it is not necessary to mention all these particulars, the street shows for itself. You see those *Levites* on the opposite side of the street? What a dignified air they carry!

PILGRIM. Yes; and their robes, and a good many

other things, look like the priests I saw in that gloomy city on the hill. But how is this? Here seems to be a little crook in the street.

CLERICUS. This was caused by one John Methodus, who attempted to infuse a little more life into this street. He was soon joined by one George Fervidus, when they, together, succeeded in building up this street we have now entered. This is called *Methodist avenue.*

SINCERITY. What is that large, nice building opposite to us.

CLERICUS. That is called *Arminian Hall.* It is well furnished, and will accommodate more guests than that other stern, palatial-looking building, right opposite to it, which was built by George Fervidus, and called *Calvinistic Inn.* These two men, however, worked in partnership, and succeeded in attracting more citizens, and getting a larger avenue, than even *Episcopalian street,* although it has not such a display of wealth and taste; for, as you pass along, you notice many signs of disorder, and many little buildings put up and deserted. Indeed this avenue is noted for its deserters, although they are enterprising, especially as pioneers, for which their nature and education seem best adapted.

FAITHFUL. Where does that little gate lead to?

CLERICUS. That opens into *Presbyterian Row.* Its order, you notice, is admirable, its edifices tall and grand, and it is said that Mr. Pride of Life attends church regularly here. There have been some eminent men in this street; but the smoke from two furnaces have blackened some of the houses. One was called the *Arian foundry*, the other *Socinian foundry*, carried on by *Drs. Tinkle* and *Knowall.* (1 Cor. xiii. 1.) The organizers of these establishments claim that *Immanuel* is only a man. Also, that when a man dies, he dies soul, body, and spirit, and so remains till the general resurrection.

SINCERITY. I wonder what they would do with the case of the rich man, and Lazarus, the thief on the cross, etc.?

CLERICUS. This queer-looking, drab-colored street, is called *Quaker street*, built by *George Fox.*

PILGRIM. Truly, it is queer-looking—houses all one story, and without windows. What can this mean?

CLERICUS. The people here are a little odd, and love candle-light better than sun-light, and don't need windows. And as they sit brooding over the moths and insects that flutter in their candle-light, they have conjured up strange vagaries, until, as improvements on candles and lamps advanced, a *gas factory* was established by a namesake of the founder, in the city of *Rochester*, by which a more brilliant, *internal* light was given, that even done away with the *sun* itself. No music is ever heard in this street. They have no use for generals, or lawyers, nor poor-houses.

FAITHFUL. Your city, sir, is truly made up of wonders. What can that mean?—a street surrounded by water, and yet looking so nice!

CLERICUS. That is *Baptist street*, the founder of

6*

which is doubtful, some claiming that *John* the *Baptist* founded it; others, that it was more recently built.

SINCERITY. There seem to be several little bridges, and then a number of alleys over there.

CLERICUS. That bridge connects with *Calvinian Row*, the other with *Arminian street.* That alley near the middle is occupied by some who will keep the seventh day of the week. That one, a little wider, is called *Free-will* alley—one *Bunyan*, to whom pilgrims are very much indebted, lived in that street; and it is said when *Mr. Restorer* came in sight of this street, he at once waded over into it, refusing to cross either of the bridges. He at first thought the plan a good one; but being of an unusually enterprising turn, he soon found the streets too narrow, and other faults, which soon led to difficulty. So, having examined the city all round, and marked with his eagle eye all its defects, he went on to the house *Beautiful*, which you see at the further end, a little beyond Baptist street, but still surrounded by water.

PILGRIM. I should like, now, to pursue my journey, and take that house in my way.

Clericus wished them to take a few turns more, and said he was sorry they had not time to view the whole, as there were many curiosities to be seen in around it—many little lanes, curiously turning off into the country. Seeing the pilgrims noticing how curiously two lanes—one coming from *Arminian Row*, the other from *Calvinistic street*—came together outside of the city, and then spread out into the country, he said, this is called *Universalian Heath.* The younger *Socinius* (Faustus) built on this heath. He was very profligate in his early life, and began to build by denying the *Trinity*, then the personality of the devil, the depravity of man, and finally, the eternity of punishment. Others have builded until, although it bears no spiritual fruits, yet it has many comforts to the souls of those who want to get to the *Celestial city*, without passing along the King's highway. Night having again interrupted their walk through the city, the pilgrims consented to the pressing, but polite, invitation of Clericus, to turn in and tarry with him till the next day. When Sincerity said he could but admire, and contrast their host with the citizens in the different streets, expressing his feeling thus:

"You different sects, who all declare,
Lo! Christ is here, or Christ is there,
Your better proofs (divinely) give,
And show me where the Christian lives."

CHAPTER VII.

THE PILGRIMS GO ON TO THE HOUSE BEAUTIFUL—INCIDENTS BY THE WAY—THEIR ENTERTAINMENT—MAGNITUDE AND BEAUTY OF MR. RESTORER'S PLAN—THE TERRIBLE EFFECTS OF SECTARIANISM.

For while one saith I am of Paul, and another, I am of Apollos, are ye not carnal and walk as men.—1 COR. iii. 4.

IN the morning the Pilgrims addressed themselves to their journey, wondering in themselves at the things they had seen, yet they felt that it had prepared them in various ways to keep the King's highway. They saw the danger of diverging even a little, and the sad effects of divisions among Christians. That it had thrown the world into distraction, and was a source of reproach to the cause of Immanuel. And Sincerity remembered that in the days of good old Bunyan, two lions were chained along near here, and wondered within himself whether the inhabitants of the city of Orthodoxy might not have fed them some, and they looked anxiously, lest, peradventure, they might spring upon them unawares, for they had heard that they were still alive when this man Restorer passed along, although in their dotage, and could not use their teeth or claws, only howl and hinder him from many of the steepled palaces they saw on the various streets. All this, however, while it kept him in the highway, served to hasten his journey to the house Beautiful, and to the Delectable mountains. Faithful, too, seemed pondering similar thoughts, yet showed by his resolute countenance that he meant to keep the King's highway. (1 John v. 4.) When Pilgrim, too, feeling a pressure of spirits, began to sing, joined by the others—

"Go on, you Pilgrims, while below,
In the sure paths of peace,
Determined nothing else to know
But Jesus and his grace.

"Observe your leader, follow Him,
He through this world has been,
Oft times reviled, but like a lamb,
Did ne'er revile again."

Thus they went on singing this beautiful song, until they came to a turning on the left hand side of the road, where a company had assembled from the different streets of the city and were earnestly talking about *Mr. Restorer*. Seeing the Pilgrims approaching with such a firm step along that way, judged they might stop at the house *Beautiful*. Whereat the mayor of the city, *Mr. Orthodox*, who was one of the company, remarked,—

ORTHODOX. Good morning, gentlemen. You seem to be going to yonder house. I am informed by these gentlemen that you were looking through our city yesterday, could you not find a place to suit you? Certainly among the various streets, you might find a home, however peculiar your notions may be. As for this man whom Clericus may have mentioned to you, we consider that he is not orthodox; that he has denied our faith and is worse than an infidel.

FAIR-SPEECH. Yes, he is a pestilent fellow; he neither regards our laws or customs; but does all he can to fill the minds of the citizens with disloyal notions, which he calls "the Bible interpreted according to the proper laws of language, the only rule of faith and practice," doing away with the names and titles in our city, and many like hurtful things.

LOVE-OF-WORLDLY-HONOR. I have heard him myself say that the honorable titles of many of our most esteemed citizens, such as Rev. D. D., etc., together with many of our customs and doings, were wrong and ought to be done away with.

SUPERSTITION. Yes, and he moreover charges much of our experiences, impressions and beliefs to the influence of early education, and says nothing is of authority in religion but what is found in the Bible.

BLIND MAN. I see clearly that this man is a heretic; I hate the very sight of him. He even charges that there is a veil over our faces, or that we see things so and so because our fathers did; so no good can come of talking with him, save to darken counsel with words.

HATE LIGHT. Even that is not all, for he is certainly possessed of one grace, that is the *gift of tongue*, and so well skilled is he in the use of this little member that he will make you believe a crow is white if you listen to him, and my advice to you is to keep out of his company.

BIGOTRY. He is more than semi-infidel, and deserves to be burnt at the stake, which I find is the only way to stop his prating about the sacred customs and traditions of these different streets.

ORTHODOX. Yes, the honor of our King is at stake, or as the Scriptures say (Acts xix. 27), "This our craft is in danger." The peace of our city is disturbed, and we are likely to be called to account for many of our venerable customs, and we have met in harmony to consult as to the common safety.

FAITHFUL. Gentlemen, it seems to me the tone and tenor of your remarks, savors more of panic and malice than that charity that hopeth for the best, and bespeaks a lack of confidence in the policy of your city and its walls of defence. It is true, we have been looking through your city, and so far from being satisfied to locate there, we think you have just grounds to fear, because as we were reading in this report of the *ouranographers,* we saw this striking passage, "For while one saith I am for Paul, and another, I am for Apollos, are ye not carnal and walk as men?" Now, we are on our way from the city of Destruction to the city of Refuge, and we wish to redeem the time; moreover, we were alarmed also when we learned that "if we walk after the flesh, (were carnal) we should die." We desire, therefore, to keep the King's highway. (2 Jo. vi.; Jo. xiv. 6.)

SINCERE. My brethren, I fear we are losing precious time to reason with these men; I prefer to be going. So they proceeded till they came to a road that led off to the left, where they saw a well looking man whose name they learned was *Fear*.

Good morning, gentlemen, said he, you seem to be going to yonder house. Are you aware of the danger that awaits you on the road? Just beyond that beautiful grove lives old *Mr. Prejudice*, who is a bitter enemy to all true pilgrims, and always sets his dogs on them, and delights in worrying them; wherefore I advise you to turn down this beautiful lane and so pass around.

PILGRIM. But is not this the direct road to the house *Beautiful?*

FEAR. Yes, but why should men run into danger when there is no need of it. A man named Nicodemus (Jo. iii. 2), first opened this lane, that prudent ones might pass in safety and give no occasion to stir up the dogs of old *Prejudice*. As it is written, "If ye be persecuted in one city flee ye to another." That is, if you cannot get along peaceably in one way, go another.

SINCERE. Sir, the point being settled that this is the right road, we shall take it and leave your pleasant by-paths for those of your stripe. It is high time that all such time-serving spirits as you are should be thrust aside, and your by-ways shut up that pilgrims be no longer bewildered and turn aside from the true and right way marked out by the good Prince, and leading directly from the city of Destruction to the city of Refuge.

FEAR. My brethren, let us be going, for I see old *Prejudice* looking at us from behind the grove, and calling out his dogs.

So they went straight forward, and to their surprise, although they were much frightened at the ado the old man made, yet the dogs seemed not to regard him, and quite refused to bite the Pilgrims, whereat old *Prejudice* raved frantically, and was ready to kill his dogs; but they were now as ready to show their teeth at him as at the strangers. So *Pilgrim* said, he wondered at it, and would like to know the reason. *Sincere* said he should inquire when they arrived at the house *Beautiful*, peradventure they might learn the reason.

They then went on with a lighter heart, and soon drew near to the house, when they discovered it was much thronged, and seeing the porter standing by the door, *Pilgrim* drew near and inquired:

PILGRIM. Sir, we are Pilgrims, bound for the city of Refuge, and hearing the fame of your house, have called to inquire whether you have room to entertain us, as we see you already have much company, and we would not be burdensome.

WATCHFUL. Burdensome! no. The good man of the house does not feel himself burdened with such pilgrims as desire such entertainment as his house affords. His stores are ample and free, and you are right welcome, come in, therefore, and partake of all his house can afford.

So the pilgrims entered and were graciously received by Christiana, the amiable companion of Mr. Restorer, by whom they were ushered into the presence of *Mr. Restorer* and his venerable father who still lingered on the shores of time, and was as lively to entertain Pilgrims as in youth.

Here, too, they found many guests from the city of *Orthodoxy* and other portions of the country. These, after partaking of the rich repast "of wine on the lees well refined" (Isa. xxv. 6), arose to depart, and seeing them going in the direction of the residence of *Mr. Prejudice*, *Sincere* watched eagerly to see what the dogs would do, and was surprised to find that they lay still in their kennels. *Old Prejudice*, however, raved and wished the house was burned and the guests too, but seemed to have lost his control over the dogs, whereat Sincere asked *Mrs. Christiana* the reason.

Ah, sir! said she, it was not always so, but of late the unprejudiced portion of the city of Orthodoxy, and the surrounding country, have made free to call and partake of our entertainments, and finding them so much better and more bountiful than they expected, they have taken portions with them and occasionally thrown fragments to the dogs, or shown them kindness in some other way (Rom. xii. 21), so that they know these men, and notwithstanding the spiteful endeavors of Prejudice, they refuse to molest them. They had been feeding them this morning and this was the reason they did not disturb you, and indeed, your own straight forward course was the safest, for "when a man's ways please the Lord, he maketh even his enemies to be at peace with him." (Prov. xvi. 7.)

FAITHFUL. We do feel reproved for listening one moment to that *Fear*, whom we met on the road, and encouraged to be faithful, and now, by your permission, we would like to take a look at this house.

But *Christiana,* ever watchful and attentive to the comforts of her guests, discovered that they were weary and needed refreshment, so she directed her daughters, Charity, Prudence, Piety and Benevolence, to prepare the supper as the day was far spent, and insisted that they should repose for the night, and then they should see the house. Supper being promptly announced, all proceeded to the dining-room, when the Pilgrims noticed that they arranged themselves around the table in a standing posture, behind their chairs, and waited in respectful silence while the master of the house, *Mr. Restorer,* in a solemn and touching manner, invoked the Divine blessing. After which, even the pleasures of the well filled board to a good appetite rendered more acute by long abstinence, hard labor and excitement, tempted by the hospitable attentions of *Mrs. Christiana* and her daughters, were lost sight of in the pleasures the soul felt as it feasted on the words that fell from the lips of the master of the house and his aged sire, until the Pilgrims began to suspicion why it was called *Beautiful.*

Supper being ended, they repaired to the sitting-room, where the conversation was continued till, ere they were aware of the flight of time, the hour for retiring arrived, when there was a lull in their talk; then the children, one by one, repeated some precious portions of Scripture, with which their minds were well stored, when the venerable *Olympus* led the worship in most piously eloquent, yet touching and simple, effusions of prayer and thanksgiving for mercies past, earnest deprecations for sins, and supplications for continued grace and mercies, especially begging that all pilgrims might be *one* in spirit, aim and effort, to glorify God and bless humanity.

After which, one of the servants, Hospitality, conducted the Pilgrims to the chamber of Promise, where they saw most comfortable couches spread, inviting to sweet repose; over one they saw written in golden letters, "Come unto me all ye that labor and I will give you rest." Over another, "All scripture given by inspiration of God, is profitable for doctrine, reproof, correction, instruction in righteousness that the man of God may be perfect, thoroughly furnished to all good works." Another, "Your sins are all forgiven." Another, "Ye shall receive the gift of the Holy Spirit." And many others which stirred thoughts that kept them awake in spite of their weariness, till at length even Faithful sank upon a couch over which he just saw written, "The spirit indeed is willing, but the flesh is weak." Sincerity turned to another, when strange and happy thoughts of what they had for supper filled his mind as he read over it, "Desire the sincere milk of the world, that ye may grow thereby." (1 Pet. ii. 2.) "Keep the feast with the unleavened bread of sincerity and truth." (1 Cor. v. 8.) While Pilgrim lay his weary body upon another, over which was written, "My grace shall be sufficient for you." (2 Cor. xii. 9.) And soon all were wrapped in sweet slumbers. So complete was the dominion of Morpheus, that ere the strange spell was broken, and they released from the arms of sleep, the grey dawn was streaking the east, when they seemed to hear a sweet voice saying, just under the window, "He giveth his beloved sleep" (Ps. cxxvii. 2), when, instantly, a thousand feathered warblers made the air vocal with notes of praise. And, on arising and going forth, they found *Mr. Restorer* already pacing to and fro along the graveled walks, amidst the beautiful trees of his garden, in deep meditation, by whom they were saluted with many inquiries as to how they rested, etc. To which they replied, they were never more refreshed, that the peculiar taste of the viands they had for supper, and the impressions made upon their minds in their chambers, had given them a peculiar appetite to taste more. The odors and appearance of the garden had also filled them with peculiar emotions, and if it were agreeable, they desired to know the names of some of these beautiful trees, and the origin of the name of the house.

RESTORER. True, I have tried to nourish some of the plants of Paradise here. This is the *Balm of Gilead* (Jer. viii. 22); that is the fig-tree, whose fruit had such an effect upon *Hezekiah* (Isa. xxxviii. 21); there is a scion of the *tree of life* (Rev. ii. 7); yonder is the *Rose of Sharon* (Songs ii. 1); and the *Lily of the Valleys*. I have also obtained a few shoots of the myrrh, and spikenard, pomegranate, camphor (Songs iv. 13), whose perfume so affects the atmosphere, and here I delight to spend much of my time in sweet meditation, amidst the song of birds, while others slumber.

SINCERE. What a beautiful fountain! Was that natural, or obtained you it by artificial means?

RESTORER. That, sir, is *preternatural* (Isa. iv. 14), and here I drink and am refreshed. Would you test its virtues (Rom. x. 9), and bathe yourselves on arising? for all my guests that do this are refreshed. (Matt. ix. 29.)

This the pilgrims found to be true; and after they had drank, they passed on a little further, and came to a beautiful little octagonal building, with the windows in the top, letting the light in from above. This proved to be the studio, or library, on entering which they were entertained with a view of the *Restorer's* plan.

RESTORER. Gentlemen, I perceive you are pilgrims. Going on pilgrimage is a great matter. The reasons for it are sufficient to move every one. I once lived in the city of Destruction, and, like you, became convinced that it would be destroyed, in consequence of its inhabitants having raised the standard of rebellion against the Divine Government. I also became satisfied of the goodness, mercy, and justice of the Great Prince; so I fled, first to the city of Orthodoxy. There I began to interest myself in every pilgrim that I saw passing the streets; and feeling that it was a matter of common and terrible interest, I feared the inhabitants of the old city were not sufficiently and properly aroused, and that the inhabitants on the various streets in Orthodoxy were not sufficiently interested and united in their efforts to save them, and maintain the authority and honor of the *Good Prince.* I commenced making inquiries, and, to my chagrin, I found my fears too true; each street seemed to have set up a little government of its own, which they seemed more intent on maintaining, and building up and adorning, than in submitting to the *orders* of the Prince and enlarging the borders of his government, and saving the inhabitants of the doomed city. I then turned my attention to the walls of the city of *Orthodoxy.* These I found, to my surprise and alarm, quite insufficient and dilapidated; in fact, in many places already fallen down, and so exposed that an enemy might easily march through them, while the very location of the gates were with difficulty found. Moreover, the drains and sewers of the city were inadequate to conduct off the refuse, and clogged at that, with the offal of their tables. (1 Cor. iii. 4.) And that the streets had been started so crookedly, that in attempts to straighten or widen them, new streets and lanes had been added in endless confusion, so that pilgrims were in danger of losing themselves altogether.

I felt fully alarmed and aroused—thought something must be done. I had many warm talks with one Clericus, and although at times he seemed sensible of the difficulties and dangers, yet he thought the walls might be patched, the streets straightened, the sewers opened, and then, by having some large *parks,* or breathing-places, where the people might assemble together and ventilate more, the health of the city would be better, the defences sufficient; and then let all the city *councils* assemble, and adopt some directions to put on guide-boards, to be put up in all parts of the city, and pilgrims might find their way with safety. Not being satisfied with this, I set myself diligently to search what might be done. Sleep almost departed from my eyes. I took special interest in the volume of reports by the *ouranographers;* these I searched diligently. And how was my alarm increased as the conviction forced itself upon my mind that the walls and streets were all wrong (1 Cor. i. 10); that the Prince had even forbidden them (Rom. xi. 17); that he had laid out a street (Jo. xiv. 6), established a city (Col. i. 18), with its defences, and ordered that the citizens should spend their time only in warning the inhabitants of the doomed city (Matt. xxviii. 19), and preparing them for the city of Refuge. And that he had forbidden them to add a single street. (Col. i. 8.) I at once proposed to desert the whole city of *Orthodoxy*, remove its walls, vacate its streets, obliterate many of its finest monuments, and demolish many of its loftiest palaces, such as the ones built by Arminius, Calvin, the Thirty-nine, on *Presbyterian Row*, and many others, and all unite to build on the one foundation laid by the Prince. (1 Cor. iii. 11.)

This created a great hum throughout the city, and finding my plan could not be carried out here, I was soon driven from the city, and came on and built here. Why our humble abode should be called *Beautiful*, I know not, unless it is because of our attempts to restore the original orders of the Prince, to build up the waste places of Zion that are fallen down, and set up the gates thereof. Many attempts have been made at *reformation*, but we only aim at *restoration*, being abundantly satisfied with the plan, building, law and order of the Church, as Christ made it, and think that no substitute or attempt at improvement could equal in beauty the original. "Beautiful for situation, the joy of the whole earth, is Mount Zion. On the sides of the north, the city of the Great King. God is known in her palaces for a refuge." (Psa. xlviii. 2.)

But, sirs, tarry with us. To-morrow is the *Lord's Day*, and in the mean time you can see more of the curiosities of the place.

CHAPTER VIII.

AMPLITUDE OF THE PROVISIONS OF THE GOSPEL SHOWN IN THE THINGS THEY SAW AT THE HOUSE BEAUTIFUL—SIMPLICITY AND SUBLIMITY OF WORSHIP WHEN STRIPPED OF WORLDLY ATTIRE AND CONFORMED TO THE GOSPEL STANDARD—THEY PROCEED ON THEIR JOURNEY—INCIDENTS BY THE WAY.

Now I praise you, brethren, that ye remember me in all things, and keep the ordinances, as I delivered them to you.—1 COR. xi. 2.

JUST then the breakfast-bell rang, and all proceeded to the sitting-room. Books were provided, and, beginning with the oldest, and so on down to the youngest that could read, each read in turn about five verses from the Living Oracles, when a few questions were propounded to the younger members of the family, and remarks made explanatory of the history, geography, or customs of the times mentioned in the lesson, while their answers showed what wonderful fruits a consistent, faithful family-training might bear. When Father Olympas, turning to the pilgrims, said, The good book says, "Bring up your children in the nurture and admonition of the Lord." (Eph. vi. 4.)

Then, all bowing down, *Restorer* offered up their morning's sacrifice of thanksgivings for the preservations of the night and the mercies of the morning, especially invoking the spirit of grace, and love, and union upon all pilgrims, deprecating the unhappy divisions and desolations of Zion, and imploring that all might yet see eye to eye, and God yet be glorified, and the world blessed, by a united and harmonious church.

At the table the same simplicity of thanksgiving, while standing, was observed. The conversation flowed ever on heaven and divine things. After breakfast they were taken to see the curiosities of the house. This house had become the resort of many guests, who came to "talk of heaven and learn the way." Here, also, they thought of the desolations of Zion, and earnestly inquired after the divine plan, by which they might be repaired, and all the children of God united in one grand enterprise to glorify God and redeem humanity. What was their glad surprise, on going out into the hall, to meet Mr. Interpreter, with some friends, whose acquaintance Pilgrim made at the Picture-Gallery on the hill. His honest, intelligent countenance (Psa. xxxi. 16), gave Pilgrim peculiar pleasure to meet him under these circumstances, while it revived the sweet memories of the past. He felt assured that he would be of great service to them in viewing the provisions of the house, as his wise suggestions and remarks seemed to add new beauty to everything they saw. So, introducing him to his companions, they requested him to accompany them while they went to take a view of the house.

INTERPRETER. Most joyfully will I do it, brethren, for I am most happy to meet you here. Brother Pilgrim, you seem much improved, When I first saw you in company with Brother *Evangelist,* you then seemed dejected and weighed down by a heavy load upon your back. How got you rid of your burden, and what speed made you hither? Fell you not into the slough of *Despond,* or feared you not the lions by the way? Saw you not Giant Despair, and were you not startled by Giant Grim?

PILGRIM. Blessed be Immanuel, that Brother *Evangelist* happened in my way. At mention of his name how many happy thoughts arise! Had it not been for him, I know not but I should have fallen into the *slough.* But, as it was, I passed safely around it by following his directions. (1 Pet. i. 5.) As to the lions and giants, they are either removed, or so closely confined that they gave us but little anxiety.

SINCERE. And we bless Immanuel, too, that the

light grows brighter and brighter. (Prov. iv. 18.) But we were promised a view of this house, and I am anxious to see what there may be here that will be serviceable to us on our journey.

INTERPRETER. As Moses, the friend of God, received in the mount a pattern by which to set up the tabernacle and arrange the Jewish worship, and was admonished to proceed according to it (Ex. xxv. 9), so may you here see that which will be of service to you.

They then proceeded to the cellar. Here were vast stores of meats and fruits (2 Cor. ix. 10), which, like the widow's barrel of meal and cruse of oil (1 Kings xvii. 14), was ever increasing, so that there was no fear of want. (Psa. xxxiv. 10.) From thence they passed up to the chambers. These were exceedingly pleasant (2 Cor. i. 20) and ample; connected with each was a nice little alcove (Matt. vi. 6), provided with inviting seats and nice windows, opening upon the most beautiful scenery, all of which was arranged in the most wonderful manner to invite meditation. (Heb. iv. 13.) They first entered the chamber of love. This was well and richly furnished (Jo. xiv. 15), and everything in order. Next adjoining this was the chamber of joy, with capacious windows overlooking a fair landscape towards the east, into which the golden rays of the sun poured their soft splendors. (1 Cor. 13.) Also, still above this was the chamber of hope (1 Pet. i. 2, 3), whose beauties seemed to fill them with peculiar emotions. On one side, full in the blaze of the rising sun, hung a magnificent picture, in a gilt frame, representing the good Prince, in shining apparel, surrounded with a halo of glory, ascending, as it were, into the air, while beneath him was an open grave, and around him a prostrate group of terror-stricken soldiers. (Jo. xviii. 6.) This so animated Faithful, that he burst out singing, joined by the others—

"Morning breaks upon the tomb,
Jesus scatters all its gloom.
Day of triumph through the skies,
See the glorious Saviour rise.

"Ye who are of death afraid,
Triumph in the scattered shade,
Drive your anxious cares away,
See the place where Jesus lay.

"Christian, dry your flowing tears,
Chase your unbelieving fears,
Look on his deserted grave,
Doubt no more his power to save."

Over this chamber was a famous observatory, from which could be seen the *Delectable Mountains*, and even the gates of the celestial city.

Interpreter led the way up a convenient flight of stairs, and as they stood gazing with rapturous delight, in the clear horizon that surrounded them, at these distant objects, he pointed them to the way (2 Pet. i. 5) which they saw clearly coming from the little wicket gate at which they had entered, leading along on the *Delectable Mountains* and quite to the shining gates of the celestial city. (Rom. ii. 7.) The country was indeed beautiful to behold, abounding with groves and orchards and vineyards; beautiful flowers and bubbling fountains. This was called *Immanuel's land*, and, said *Interpreter*, as you pass through this country, you will be made welcome to all that it affords. There, too, you will find kind shepherds tending their flocks, from whom you may learn many things that will be useful to you on your journey.

They then descended to the armory. Here they saw every kind of weapons and armor, offensive and defensive. (Eph. vi. 11.) *Interpreter* said it was necessary they should be fully equipped, as they would have use for all these things. So they were all completely harnessed from head to foot. And so seeing and talking, the time passed rapidly by, and ere they were aware, the day had passed, and right willing were they to repose again in the chamber where they had rested so sweetly the night before; and now so full were their minds of the things they had seen that their dreams were most pleasing, and surely time must have fled with magic speed on velvet feet, for the first return of consciousness was produced by sweet voices singing; and listening they caught these words:

CHRIST the Lord has risen to-day
Sons of men and angels say,
Raise your joys and triumphs high,
Sing you heav'ns, and earth reply.

Love's redeeming work is done—
Fought the fight—the battle won—
Lo! the sun's eclipse is o'er,
Lo! he sets in blood no more.

Vain the stone, the watch, the seal,
Christ has burst the gates of hell.
Death in vain forbids his rise,
Christ has opened Paradise.

And while this beautiful song proceeded, they arose and found the family already assembled for morning worship. After the usual repast, they repaired to the rural but ample and tasty chapel near, on the banks of a beautifully meandering stream, and found the children in throngs, assembled to spend the earlier hours of the day in studying the Living Oracles, their smiling faces and cheerful voices showed that they enjoyed the morning school, and their ready answers told that they were early learning to prize and store the lessons of sacred history imparted by their superintendents and teachers, and ere they had finished, the people began to assemble from the surrounding country, until the house was filled. And songs of praise from the congregation soon took the place of juvenile hum and joy. This continued till the venerable Pastor entered the house, who proved to be Mr. Restorer, and entering the pulpit proceeded to read this beautiful hymn:

"Hail morning, known among the blest,
Morning of hope and joy and love,
Of heavenly peace and holy rest,
Pledge of the endless rest above."

Which was sung by the congregation, after which he read from the Scriptures an account of the resurrection. Then, after prayer and singing another hymn, he proceeded to say that the Bible was one of the most wonderful of books; that it was a book composed of *sixty-six* books, written by some *fifty* different authors, during a period of 1600 years, and yet it was the most plain and harmonious of all books. It was divided, first, into *Old* and *New Testament*. The Old contained an account of two *dispensations*. The first, called the Patriarchal, extending from Adam to Moses. The second, called the Jewish, or National, extending from Moses, the law-giver, to the Messiah. The New, contained an account of the third and last, or Christian dispensation. The first, he styled the *starlight*, the second, the *moonlight*, the third, the *sunlight* ages of the world. That Messiah was the sun of this last, in whose resplendent rays all others were absorbed like the stars before the rising sun. That we were now as dependent on the New Testament for light, on all spiritual matters and duties, as we were upon the sun for light in the material world. That so perfect were its provisions, that to add to or subtract from, was to mar its beauty, and destroy its harmony, and would subject the offender to the most fearful penalty.

He closed with the most stirring exhortation to love to study and obey its dictates, that we might enjoy its promises. Then, after another song, he approached a table which stood in front of the pulpit, and, removing a napkin, revealed a loaf of bread and a vessel of wine, which its pure white folds had encircled. He said, moreover, that in the Jewish worship, which was a type of the Christian, they had twelve loaves, representing their twelve tribes. These were placed upon the table in their temple by the Priests, and renewed once every week (Lev. xxiv. 8), and eaten by the Priests. But now, as there was to be but one body (1 Cor. xii. 12), and all true believers were to be one in that body (Eph. iv. 16), so there was to be but *one* loaf in a congregation, to represent the one body. (1 Cor. xii. 5.) That, as it was in the temple of the Lord, all that were truly in Christ had access to this loaf and wine, and were to approach it on the first day of the week. (Acts xx. 7.) If every week had a first day, then they were to approach it *every week*. The bread was then broken, with thanksgiving (1 Cor. x. 16), and the wine likewise, and distributed to the members, who partook of it with a simplicity which was truely sublime, while the Pilgrims were filled with new and strange, yet most pleasing emotions. Sincerity said he scarcely knew whether he was in the body or out, but never before had he witnessed anything that struck him with such force and beauty, and seemed so like what he read in the Scriptures, and in early church history. Faithful said it reminded him of the picture *Interpreter* had showed them of Moses receiving a pattern of the Tabernacle, and the directions God gave him, (Heb. viii. 5), "See thou make all things according to the pattern shown thee."

Pilgrim said it did look to him like restoring the "ancient order of things," and it struck him that the *simplicity* of the *faith* was one of its chief beauties, and that adapted it to the capacity of all as a safe and sufficient rule of *faith* and *manners*. Then having sung another hymn (Matt. xxvi. 30), the congregation dispersed.

So the day flew by while they were meditating on these things. In the evening they attended meeting again, and heard a discourse on the things pertaining to the kingdom. This tended, also, to enlighten their eyes, showing them when the kingdom was set up (Acts ii. 33), and the manner of entering into it. (Jo. iii. 5.) That it had all the elements of a perfect kingdom; hence all its laws must remain in full force till the same authority, or a higher one, should alter them, and that this government was ultimately to prevail. (Acts ii. 34.) And, in conclusion, the speaker called upon all to submit to the authority of the Good Prince, and enter at once upon his service (Acts ii. 38), when many, with streaming eyes, rose up and went forward to confess their faith in the Prince, and show their willingness to obey him, and that same hour of the night were baptized. (Acts xii. 6.)

Having enjoyed the hospitalities of the house for a few days, they essayed to go forward, when they were supplied with some of the best provisions which the house could afford, and, withal, Piety brought forth the garment of Humility, and bade them put it on (Ti. ii. 10), and, with care, it would supply the place of armor in most cases, and give them less hindrance in their journey; so, being thus furnished, they took their leave, with many expressions of gratitude for what they had received, and were especially exhorted to keep the good old way (Heb. ix. 8), called *Immanuel's path.* (Phil. i. 27.)

For some time the pilgrims proceeded in a fine, pleasant, open country, till at length they came to a large road, which turned off to the left. This road was much beaten by carriages and horses, but the direct way began here to grow narrow, and appeared not to be much traveled. At the turning of the road stood a high post, with an index pointing to the left, with this inscription: "The new road, marked out by councils, conferences, and synods, leading through the cities of Convenience, Worldly Wisdom, and Self-Conceit. But, remembering the exhortation that had been given them on setting out, they kept straight forward, but soon came to some by-roads, leading from the *straight path* to the new road, out of which came some of the inhabitants of those cities, by whom the pilgrims were grossly abused. They bore these taunts for some time with great patience, and then only replied with respectful, but firm and pointed language (Ti. i. 10); till at length, one, more insolent than the rest, gave Faithful a severe blow on the face, which so irritated him that he turned aside to chastise the offender (Jude iii.), but he, being nimble of foot, gave him a long chase through bushes and briers, which left an occasional rent in his clothes, while the inhabitants of the city of Depravity, which lay a little beyond the new road, gathered round and enjoyed the sport amazingly to see *Faithful* give the *Orthodox* such a sound drubbing, and patting him on the shoulder, told him they thought he had the best of the race, although he had got his clothes a little torn, and had lost some precious time; so they got up a little purse on the spot to make him amends, though, by this time, *Sincere* and *Pilgrim* had gotten on some distance; and now, withal, getting a little weary, they sat down by the wayside, and opening their knapsack, brought forth some of the good things given them on leaving the house *Beautiful*, and now truly found them refreshing. (Eph. vi. 18.)

SINCERE. This is, indeed, a rich repast. How thoughtful they were thus to provide for us! I would Brother *Faithful* were with us to share these dainties. It may be well, at times, to show our zeal for the truth by defending it earnestly, and even punishing an adversary with stripes, but it agrees better with my taste thus to enjoy such a repast as this.

PILGRIM. See here; this must be the work of *Mrs. Christiana*, and placed here seemingly in anticipation of such an occasion—"Study the things that make for peace, and things wherewith one may edify another." (Rom. xiv. 19.) And here is another nice roll: "But the servant of the Lord must not strive, but be gentle towards all men." (2 Tim. ii. 24.) I was also thinking of Brother *Faithful*, and wondering whether his course would be most effectual in opening the eyes of those impudent citizens. Paul was once beset in a similar manner (Acts xxiii. 3), and lost his temper, and was sorry for it, and then determined to know nothing but Christ and Him crucified. (Rom. ii. 2.)

SINCERE. Yes, and Paul fought with wild beasts at Ephesus (1 Cor. xv. 32); and since there are so many different views in the world it will produce clashing, and yet, no doubt, genders jealousies and bad feelings. But see, here is another dish—"Praying always with all prayer and supplication." (Eph. vi. 18.)

So, after they had eaten and talked for a long time, they arose and pursued their journey. They had not gone far before they espied one coming across a meadow, and approaching the road by a pleasant by-path, which, on drawing near, they found to be much beaten; so, on coming up, they were thus addressed:

FORMALITY. (For such proved to be his name. 2d Tim. iii. 5.) May I make free to inquire whither you are bound?

PILGRIM. We are fleeing from the city of Destruction to the Celestial City of Refuge.

FORMALITY. Right glad am I to meet you, for I am going there also, and shall be glad of your company, for I rather like the society of Christians, and think it well enough to go on pilgrimage.

SINCERE. But your dress does not betoken the pilgrim (1 Pet. i. 15), and as for provision (Matt. xxvi. 41), you seem not to have laid in any.

FORMALITY. I have noticed the treatment of all those who try to keep strictly to the road, and wear the odd garb of Pilgrims, and having made geography my study from my youth up, I am able to keep along these by-paths, and by conforming a little to the fashions in innocent things, enjoy the society of pilgrims, and all others too.

SINCERE. But, are we not required to separate ourselves from the world (Ti. ii. 14), because the friendship of the world is enmity against God. (Jas. iv. 4.) How, then, can any one truly loving God, enjoy the fashions, amusements, and society of the world? and is it not because of these things that relgion is at so low an ebb, and reduced to a mere profession or formality?

FORMALITY. As to that, I think if anybody has a right to be gay and joyful, it is the Christian. It is not necessary that we go drooping like a bulrush, always gloomy and sad. It is well enough to go to meeting on the Lord's day, if one feels well and is inclined to go, and also to take our seats with the members and go through the form of worship; and I don't deny but that it may be well enough to have some family religion, and even family worship, if one has time; but then I have so much on hand, and frequently have so many work-hands around, or visitors, that I don't find time to have worship; and as to giving thanks, I have not got in the way of that yet.

SINCERE. And you profess to be a pilgrim, going to the Celestial City. Why man, can you be in earnest! is religion a matter of *convenience* and *inclination*? Is there not a greater interest at stake than in any worldly business, and then to say nothing about *religious order* being a real saving of time if it is a reality, would not our love for it, and our pleasure in it, prompt us at once to invite our work-hands and visitors, too, to pause at the family altar and enjoy a repast so sweet. And, as to thanksgiving, what sin so inexcusable and unnatural as ingratitude. The world's scorn rests upon the ungrateful, to say nothing of the impudence of receiving daily and hourly blessings without thankfulness.

FORMALITY. Oh! as to that I feel thankful enough, and the Lord knows all of that, if I do not tell him so; and then, I am a little diffident, and havn't a gift to express my feelings in ideas and words, and so I don't think it necessary.

SINCERE. But you seem very fluent in argument, and able to express yourself on other subjects. Would you not think it very impolite to receive favors from your neighbors, and not express your gratitude to them. How would you feel if your neighbor should come daily to your orchard and granary, and take fruit and grain without either paying you a cent or thanking you; and yet, no doubt, he would feel a sort of selfish gratitude.

FORMALITY. But, my brother, if you undertake to enjoin the duty of prayer and thanksgiving on all the members of the church, you will cut off and keep out a good many that would be honorable members, that would swell the numbers, and pay a good deal to the support of the church.

PILGRIM. I have been listening to this discussion with much interest, for it seems to me to be one of importance. We have learned some things about the Celestial City, to which we desire to go, and where we expect to live for ever, and that without these habits we could not be happy there; nay, the Good Prince intimated (Matt. xvii. 21) that we can only get rid of the spirits of this world by *prayer* and *fasting*. That everything we enjoy is sanctified by prayer. (1 Tim. iv. 5.) Therefore, we cannot live, even here, as Christians, without prayer, much less could we get to heaven, or enjoy it without prayer.

Prayer is the Christian's native breath,
The Christian's vital air;
His watchword at the gate of death,
He enters heaven by prayer.

Now, if these things be so, those that live prayerless lives must be dry, dead, or rotten members of the church, and the honor and support the church will receive from them will be proportional blight and ruin. Religion is brought into disrepute, the church corrupted, and their own souls ruined in the end.

God has also threatened the most dreadful calamities upon those families that do not have family worship, and now, if it does not come in some terrible form, then this threat must fail; so *Mr. Formality*, look well to yourself, and all that follow your example.

FORMALITY. Well, I am not disposed to be querulous, so if I cannot walk with you and enjoy my liberty without being reproved, I can go on alone.

CHAPTER IX.

THE PILGRIMS PASS THE VALLEY OF HUMILITY—EXPERIENCE JOINS THEIR COMPANY—VARIOUS INCIDENTS, SHOWING THE DANGER OF FORMALITIES—COURSE AND THE NECESSITY OF A DEEP AND THOROUGH WORK—THEY REACH THE VALLEY OF THE SHADOW OF DEATH—ENTER INFIDEL HALL.

We have, also, a more sure word of prophecy, whereunto ye do well that ye take heed, as unto a light that shineth in a dark place, until the day dawn, and the day-star arise in your hearts.—2 PETER i. 19.

Now it was evident that Formality was, after all, shaping his sails more to catch the popular breeze, or to sail with the current, rather than from any thorough estimate *of*, or love *for*, religion, and that his relish for the society of the pilgrims grew less in proportion as it required the performance of duties that involved the affections. (Col. ii. 3.) And, having made his *inclinations* the standard, he was ready to leave their company whenever any little occasion offered, or to betray the religion he *professed*, merely whenever a demand should be made upon his purse, or life, that involved a heart-attachment. Evidently his affections were not set upon things above; so that, instead of laying up treasure in heaven (Matt. vi. 20), he evidently preferred to keep his treasure on earth.

They had not proceeded far on their journey till they entered a settlement that had evidently been made a long time, as the inhabitants were very numerous, and everything bore the marks of age, and also of decay. This arrested the attention of Sincere, who said:

SINCERE. I see here many tokens of Christian civilization, but no school-houses, or churches; the children seem rude, uncombed, and ragged; the fences are decaying, the roads and bridges neglected, and houses going to ruin; certainly, something must be wrong.

FORMALITY. Yes, I was acquainted with some that came and settled here. They had Christian parents and a Christian education, but concluded they themselves could get along without it; but, certainly, they ought to maintain self-respect enough to keep things up, and appear clean and tasty; and, as for schools and churches, they give an air of prosperity, and the people ought to have pride enough to keep them up.

SINCERE. So, Brother Formality, you see that Christianity does make a difference; and, if it makes a difference for the better, it must be a reality. If a reality, it presents a deep cause for even earthly prosperity, since it purifies the heart, elevates the affections, and refines the whole being, by presenting motives high as heaven and lasting as eternity. As to self-respect, none truly respect themselves who do not respect God, and schools and churches are simply aids to improve the mind and cultivate the soul, and, instead of giving an *air* of prosperity, they are the mainsprings of all improvements, and should be maintained from a sense of highest duty and greatest pleasure. Little do the infidel world realize to what an extent they are indebted to Christianity for all the improvements and benefits of society; and, so far from getting along without it, the world would go to heathenism and ruin.

While thus discoursing, Pilgrim descried, a little distance to the left, a group of houses, built along a crooked and disorderly street, thronged with a similar looking set of loungers, whiling away the time, drinking and smoking, in idle sports and blasphemy; while the children, with stumps of cigars, were rapidly learning the same thriftless lessons.

PILGRIM. When I lived in the city of Destruction, I noticed that these habits generally went together. True, there were some that used tobacco that wanted to be more respectable than to swear and drink, but so universally was it practised by the former class, that it became their *badge*, and hence even respectable men were suspicioned if they used this *badge;* and there was some grounds for it, since what was such a universal favorite with all of vitiated appetites, cannot be safe for a good man to practise. To say the least, it is an unclean habit, fit only for unclean places and persons. And, in all such cases, it affords a very good chance for all who wish to be pure (1 Tim. v. 22), to separate themselves (2 Cor. vi. 17), to crucify the flesh, with its affections and lusts. (Gal. v. 24.)

SINCERE. I think, Brother Pilgrim, although you may be justly severe, yet you are in danger of offending many good, pious brethren, and even *sisters*, who have long been in the habit of using tobacco. I have no defence to make of the practice, yet it has become so general, one is liable to lose popularity by opposing it, and you know we are commanded to study the things that make for peace (Rom. xiv.), and things wherewith one may edify another.

PILGRIM. Very true; but are we to expect peace at the expense of purity? (Jas. iv. 17.) He is not the safest friend who would refrain from reproving us of a fault, for fear of offending. I know this habit is very wide-spread, and, although it may not be the smoke of the *bottomless pit*, yet it ascends up for ever and ever; and, although it was scarcely known 300 years ago, when the race was much healthier than now, yet many, and even some *Physicians*, now think it is good for the health, notwithstanding it induces nervousness, dyspepsia, and even *delirium tremens*. And, so long as the love of popularity, or fear of offending, governs the tongue, sin will go unreproved, and piety be sickly.

FORMALITY. Brethren, I think such discussions are unprofitable so long as these things are practised by *saint* and *sinner;* the best plan is to allow every one to be fully persuaded in his own mind, and then do as they think proper. Let us try and encourage a decent respect to the forms and ceremonies of religion, and not be fastidious about these minor matters. But see here, the straight road leads down yon hill into a low, gloomy country, that affords but little to cheer the heart.

SINCERE. Are you acquainted with the country along there?

FORMALITY. Not from personal experience; but I have read some about it, and, having been something of a reader, and inquisitive, I have learned of a much more pleasant and commodious road, leading around through the country of *Toleration*, where I have some relations, on my mother's side, by the name of *Self-conceit*, *Merit*, *Pharisee*, *Reputation*, *Covetousness*, and some others, any of whom would be glad to entertain us; and, although not members of the church, they are of good repute, especially from those that are without.

PILGRIM. What are the names of these two roads, and where will they lead us to in the end?

FORMALITY. The straight road leads down into the *Valley of the Shadow of Death*, connected on the right to another, called the *Valley of Humility*. This other road, leading around on this beautiful ridge, is sometimes called the *Way of the World*, but many choose to go this road, because it is smoother, and wide enough for carriages, and better shaded, so that the sun does not beat down so hot; and it is claimed they both lead to the Celestial City.

SINCERE. See, yonder comes our good Brother *Faithful*, covered with dust and sweat. So, then, he has got through with his struggle, and I hope will still be of great service to us by the experience he has gained in his recent encounter, for we know not with whom we may meet in the valley before us, for its name does not savor of a flowery path.

FORMALITY. It is he indeed, and he seems to have a companion.

FAITHFUL. So, ho! my brethren. I am glad to find you. This is my friend *Experience*, who came up with me on the road. He seems to be somewhat acquainted with the country, and has given me much valuable information, and may be of service to us all. But who is this, and why are you halting by the way?

PILGRIM. This is Mr. *Formality*, who joined us at the cross-road you may have noticed some distance back, and we were just talking about those two roads. Brother Formality thinks we had better take that one, which he says leads around this gloomy valley. Perhaps Brother Experience could tell us which we had better take.

EXPERIENCE. It is not my custom to say much about a road beforehand, but, if you wish, I will accompany you along either.

FAITHFUL. Although my good brother, *Experience*, is not much of a prophet, yet he is good company, and makes many things plain as we go along and inspires one with hope (Rom. v. 4) and courage. As to this companion of yours, *Formality*, he seems to be intelligent and respectable in appearance, but I begin to suspicion his being a safe guide, for his counselling you to take a roundabout road, for the sake of ease and pleasure, since it may lead you wide of the mark (Matt. vii. 13), and leave you in the open country of ruin, instead of leading to the *Celestial City*. And as we have sufficient warnings and instructions about the way, I am in favor of taking the straight forward one, let it lead us through ever so deep valleys, or over ever so high mountains, providing it brings us all right at last.

FORMALITY. Gentlemen, you can take your choice. I shall do as I have a mind to. As to religion, I do not think it demands such exposures and hardships, in rather an unfrequented country where there are so few conveniences and pleasures.

EXPERIENCE. I have learned, brethren, that the path of duty is always the safest, and when we go forward with resolution, it is the easiest and happiest, and brings all right in the end.

SINCERE. I am with Brother *Faithful* in his decision to take the right road, whether there are the conveniences or pleasures, Brother *Formality* speaks of, or not, since, if they are to be purchased at the expense of duty, they can neither be satisfying or honorable. Evidently, the condition of the settlement we have just passed, is the result of seeking pleasure at the expense of duty; moreover, I am satisfied *Formality* prefers this pleasant road because it leads around the cross of duty (Matt. x. 38), and fears it may cost him a few pennies if we should have to put up at the Hotel of *Mr. Philanthropist*, or the Inns of Charity and Benevolence, and especially as this road through the valley is said to lead past Immanuel's Custom-House, where all true Pilgrims call to "*render unto God the things that are God's.*" (Matt. xxii. 21.)

While this discussion was pending, *Formality* turned away from them into the road leading off to the left, saying, as he did so, I shall do as I please with my own and take my risks for the outcome, while the pilgrims proceeded straight forward, and sure enough soon found themselves on the brow of a hill from which they could see some distance along the road *Formality* had taken, and where they saw many stately mansions and glittering carriages filled with passengers in gaudy apparel, and unto which they saw *Formality* bowing with many abject tokens of respect, hoping thereby to gain their favor and get a chance to ride with them to enjoy their company.

EXPERIENCE. Immanuel once stood here, and as he stood here (Matt. iv. 3), looking with intense anxiety and grief on the folly of those who chose that road, the rebel prince himself came to him and told him that all the country along that road belonged to him, with all its palaces, and fine equipage, and that if he would consent to travel that road, he would put it all under his control, and that he could live in ease and honor ever after.

PILGRIM. Truly, that was a tempting offer.

EXPERIENCE. Tempting to whom it may be tempting, but Immanuel was then laying out this very road that we are in, in order to afford a passage for pilgrims to the Celestial City, and knew that that other road would never take them there, and since this was a matter of infinitely more importance and value (Matt. xvi. 26) than all the wealth and pleasures along the other road, it did not prevail a moment with him, so he kept on, and the result is, he laid out this road that, although just here it descends rapidly, and in other places is rather steep, and even leads through some gloomy places, yet it is entirely safe; has good accommodations, abundantly supplied with fruit all along (Jo. iv. 14), and living springs of water, most healthy and refreshing; moreover, it is much the shortest route, and in the end, not only brings the pilgrim to the city; but puts him in possession of nicer houses (2 Cor. v. 1), greater wealth (Matt. x. 30), and more ecstatic and lasting pleasures (Ps. xvi. 11) than he could have found on the other road.

SINCERE. Truly, Brother *Faithful*, the company of this companion you have brought with you, more than verifies your promise. (Rom. v. 4.) He fills my heart with courage and joy and inspires me with a desire to go forward.

Faithful drew his *girdle* a little tighter (1 Pet. i. 13), *Pilgrim* grasped the book he still carried, firmer (2 Pet. i. 19), *Sincere* took another sip from the bottle of milk *Mrs. Christiana* had placed in their basket, and they all set forward, passing gently down the declivity into the valley. This, *Experience* told them, was called the Vale of Humility, and notwithstanding it was, in some places, slippery and steep, and they might get some falls, yet it was safe, and all they had to do was to keep in the road and it would bring them all right at last. But as they passed on, the hills on each side seemed to grow higher and come nearer together, yet the sun beat down with unusual fervor and brilliancy, showing every spot of dirt on their clothes, but they noticed, as the sun shone a little while upon them, it fell off. Thus they proceeded until at length the hills on the south side rose so high and steep, that at times it shut out the light of the sun. These hills formed the sides of the *Valley of the Shadow of Death,* which extended for several miles. This valley, *Experience* told them, was the most difficult and dangerous part of the road, as there were many gins, and snares, and pits, and caverns all along, haunted by spectres and fiends, yet if they kept straight forward, they would pass in safety; but they must watch at all times (Matt. xxvi. 41), and if at any time they came to cross roads, or the path grew dim from the obscurity of the heavens, or the gloom of the hills or otherwise, they must examine the directions carefully, which they would find written in Pilgrim's book.

So they pressed on with what speed they could, hoping to pass this part of the valley while the sun was well up. But on a sudden, the heavens grew black as sack-cloth, and every thing seemed to indicate an approaching storm. And now they began to feel alarmed at finding themselves thus suddenly and unexpectedly overtaken with such a storm, when they seemed to be getting on so well. (1 Cor. x. 12.) At length the tempest burst upon them, attended with dreadful thunderings and lightnings, and all nature around seemed agitated, and some fears were entertained about their being able to extricate themselves. *Experience* was about to make some remarks by way of encouragement, but the tempest grew so apace, they could not hear distinctly what he said. One of them happening to look behind, thought he saw a number of frightful forms coming on rapidly after them, and he suddenly cried out for fear, when they all looked round, and seeing such a haggard troop, they were instantly deprived of all courage and began to run. But it was now so dark and their minds so confused, they took different roads. *Faithful* and *Sincere* happened to hit the right one, but *Pilgrim* and *Experience* ran off to the left, where the frowning hills seemed to bend away, leaving a more open space, but filled with brambles and a thick undergrowth which impeded their progress very much. They had not gone far, before they perceived before them what seemed a faint light. They made up to it and found it proceeded from a large house, situated on the declivity of the hill, and after searching a little they found a path leading up to the door, where they knocked and were invited to come in. Being affrighted and bewildered they accepted the invitation and entered.

EXPERIENCE. We were unexpectedly overtaken by a storm in the valley, and were seeking shelter, but little thought there could be such a building in this gloomy region. (Jo. iii. 19.) May I inquire what house this is, and if you entertain pilgrims?

I am sometimes called *Natural Man* (1 Cor. ii. 14), although I claim to believe in a *divine revelation*, in every man's own mind, or an impartation of those *divine rays* that flow from the *sun* or *fountain* of our existence, which illuminates all souls that are brought into existence. And this house is sometimes called Infidel Hall, simply because its inhabitants reject the superstitious teachings of the Bible, and trust to a clearer light, which the true God puts into the heart of every intelligent being. As to receiving pilgrims, we usually entertain those that get *bewildered* and *out of the highway*, providing they are so fortunate as to find the house, which is not always the case, since, as you have intimated, it is strangely situated. Because we prefer to be retired from the dust of the highway, and where the sun—which you may have noticed back a way—does not shine with such oppressive fervor. And hence it needs a peculiar eye to see back here in our retirement—like that of an owl or bat, who prefer to fly in the dark, and cannot see in sunlight.

Pilgrim, who stood listening to this conversation, felt a strange trembling coming over him, as he thought of the instructions of Interpreter and the warnings of Evangelist (2 Tim. ii. 26), and the incidents of the day, nor did this strange talk allay his emotions; and having some suspicions that he had heard of this hall while he lived in the city of Destruction, and that he had seen guests at the hotel where he served, from this very place, and who talked much like this man, he asked:

PILGRIM. Have you ever heard of the city of Destruction, and know you the distance of this from that place?

NATURAL MAN. Yes, sir, full well, or the place the *superstitious* vulgarly call such, although I am of a different opinion. (2 Pet. iii. 4.) The distance is not great, and there is a very smooth, nice road leading from the back of this hall, for coaches or footmen. And we hold much intercourse. They usually put up at the City Hotel, called Sensuality, kept by one Lust-of-the-Flesh, a man of much note, and who always sets a good table. And all the members of my family, and servants, are *good livers.*

PILGRIM. What are the names of some of your attendants?

NATURAL MAN. There is the lady of the house, Miss Representation, who is very talkative, and loves to entertain guests; also, Mr. Credulity, my librarian, who is a great reader, and believes in everything. Then here is Prejudice, my coachman, who always goes with me when I go abroad. He is a son of the old man who lives between the city of Destruction and Orthodoxy, and keeps a lot of dogs, which we used to employ sometimes to hunt among these mountains. Yes, and we have a constant guest here, called Sceptic, who sometimes makes himself very useful by conversing with those who are frightened about what they have seen or heard, and delights to show guests through the house.

EXPERIENCE. If you are willing, we would like to take a look through your house while the storm continues.

NATURAL MAN. By all means, sir. It is our delight thus to entertain our guests. So he called Mr. Sceptic, and requested him to show the gentlemen through the house.

Whereupon he took them to the library. Now, it so happened that, had there been no tempest and gloom without, there would have been no light from that source, since there were no windows fitted to let in the light. (Rom. i. 28.) So Sceptic carried a little *dark lantern*, which threw a glimmering light around the room, in which they saw the portraits of some special favorites. There was Epicurus and Plato, Parker and Fowler, Davis, Ballou, Barker, Fox'es, Ferguson, and many others. They saw, also, certain lewd representations, and mottoes written over them—Lust of the flesh, Lust of the eye, and Pride of life, and under them little doors, entering rooms, unto which Sceptic, pointing, said, There is nothing better than to eat, drink, and be merry, for this is all that a man hath under the sun. (Eccl. ii. 24.)

Whereat Pilgrim trembled more, and hearing the storm roar without, he said, How terrible is this place! Then said Sceptic, I once felt as you feel. I was rocked in the cradle of Orthodoxy, when my mind was filled with bugbears, which greatly troubled me, day and night; but when I grew up, I went and spent a few days in the city of Sensuality. There I heard of the fame of these great lights, and soon learned that there was no *hell*, and hearing of an opening here, I came and sought employment, as I wanted to be useful; and hearing this house was situated in such a dangerous place, it just suited my taste.

But, said Experience, I perceive that you went the wrong way in order to obtain light, and I think your history is a proof of the dangerous tendency of your doctrine. For following these great lights, as you term them, has led you into the darkest region you could find, even into the darkest corner of the *Valley of the Shadow of Death,* and this darkness, shutting out all light of the future, has left you free to indulge in all the sinful lusts and inclinations of your evil heart.

SCEPTIC. No, sir; I have only broken the shackles of early superstitious education, and learned to think for myself. As to the future, I had no hand in bringing myself into the world, and don't intend to in getting out. Therefore, the Creator can do with me as he sees fit. If there is a future state of happiness, I expect to enjoy it. But as to a personal devil or hell, these have no existence, save in our own minds, and I am glad that I have got rid of all such notions.

PILGRIM. But where are you taking us to now?

SCEPTIC. As the storm has somewhat abated, I wished to take you up on our observatory. This, you will see, is the highest point in this building. From there you can see to the utmost limits of the dominion of Mr. Infidel.

PILGRIM. I confess I am unable to see things as clearly as I could wish. I can just distinguish a dark object bounding the prospect, with a kind of inscription written over it.

SCEPTIC. Yes, that is the graveyard. That inscription reads, 'DEATH: AN ETERNAL SLEEP!" So we give ourselves no special concern about anything beyond. And these storms, that so frightened you, and scattered your company, give us no special trouble. Indeed, when any are so frightened and foolish as to join the church, or start on a pilgrimage, those difficulties that are so apt to arise, are the means of driving many back to our fellowship, and they strive to show their joy at getting back by being ten-fold worse than they were before. (Matt. xii. 41.)

EXPERIENCE. My brother, if you have now seen and heard enough, we will betake ourselves to our journey, as I perceive the storm has abated, and I am anxious for the fate of our brethren.

PILGRIM. I have, and I am most ready and anxious to be on the way, *storm* or no *storm*, rather than dwell here any longer, and am more than half convinced, after seeing and hearing these things, that the reason why any one becomes an Infidel, Sceptic, or Universalist, is because of their secret inclinings to Adam the first. (Eph. iv. 22.) And I begin to suspicion, even from one remark that Mr. Sceptic made, that this storm was sent to try our faith. (Heb. xii. 7.) How sorry I am that we became so frightened as to *turn out of the path* to seek shelter, and thus shamefully desert our brethren! How know we but they are in trouble? Why should we refuse to bear it with them, and fly from the ills we bore to those we knew not of? I am glad, my dear Brother Experience, that you are with me, and now let us strive together to get back and hunt up our brethren. I seem to have new views and feelings of the great work of reforming and redeeming the world, and feel most deeply the weight of these lines:

"Oh! my Father, cried I, inly, thou hast striven, I have willed,
Now the mission of the angel of thy patience is fulfilled.
I have tasted earthly pleasures, yet my soul is craving food;
Let the summons thou hast given to thy harvest be renewed.
I am ready now to labor—wilt thou call me once again?
I will join the willing reapers as they gather up the grain."

CHAPTER X.

THE SCATTERED COMPANY MEET AGAIN—VALLEY; WHY CALLED VALLEY OF DEATH—INCIDENTS BY THE WAY —VARIOUS DISCUSSIONS, SHOWING WHY SO FEW START, AND SO MANY FALL OUT BY THE WAY—THRILLING ADVENTURES.

For to be carnally minded is death, but to be spiritually minded is life and peace.—ROM. viii. 6.

GLAD, indeed, were the pilgrims to find themselves free from this terrible house; and, although it still seemed dark, the ground wet, and the heavens still frowning, they preferred now even to brave the storm, or any exposure, rather than abide in such a place. Experience seemed very thoughtful, and turning to Pilgrim, said, I begin to suspicion why this is called the Valley of Death. If a departure from the true path leads to death (Rom. vi. 23), then certainly the *enticements*, and *gins*, and *pitfalls* that beset this part of the road entitle it to this appellation. I remember many who ran well in the Christian career till they came here (Matt. xiii. 21); they then seem to lay down their watch, or suffer themselves to be surprised by the enemy and taken captive—and, alas! too many are willing to remain captives. I remember young Americus, a youth of noble gifts. He seemed to be getting on finely; the weather and going were peculiarly favorable for him. But even these roved his ruin, since it seemed to invite to that pleasure he could least resist. Flattered and caressed, the loins of his mind gave way. The fair daughters of the land came forth, and thoughtlessly displayed those charms which won away his heart. Instead of resisting and fleeing, he nursed his passion by familiar intercourse and foolish talk, which was contrary to the blessed precept his mother had taught him. (1 Thess. v. 22.) He seemed to lose all memory of the warnings he had received (Prov. v. 5), and all care of the terrible consequences of his crime (Rev. xxi. 8), till, in an evil hour, his feet were taken in the snare, and he perished miserably in this valley. I remember, too, the case of one *Simple,* born in the town of Avarice, and, although at times he seemed to give evidence of piety, and to express a desire to get safely to the Celestial City, yet his early education and habits were so strong, whenever a *contribution* or *subscription* for the support of the Gospel came up, that he seemed to say, I must have my religion without money and without price. He seemed to prosper in worldly business and grew rich, because he strove to get just near enough to the church and religion to receive all its benefits, yet so held himself as to refuse all its burdens, save only when it would take a few reluctant words, by way of a few remarks in meeting, or a prayer, just enough to enable him to keep his place in the church. Ever so loving a plea by a minister or agent, that ended in a call for money to sustain or spread abroad the blessed Gospel of salvation, seemed to offend him, or make him feel that if he gave any it was thrown away, and he mourned to think afterward he might have given less. His mind never fully rose above his early habits, his faith grew weaker, if possible, and heaven seemed like a *mirage*, or an intangible exaltation from the earth. I suppose he could not realize it; and so, after travelling part of the way through this valley, he came to a smooth *lane*, leading off to the left of the main road, called Dema's lane (2 Tim. iv. 10), which he took, and was never heard of more.

PILGRIM. See, my good Brother Experience, here are abundant evidence, in addition to what you have said, that this is a dangerous place. Here are many graves on the right and left of the road, and some bodies, even, that are unburied. (1 Tim. v. 6.) Let us read some of these inscriptions on these gravestones. Here is one that says, "*Wise above what is written;*" another, "One that gave heed to seducing spirits, and doctrines concerning departed spirits;" also, "One who loved pre-eminence." And, indeed, they felt very sad as they read among the cases of death in this valley—"covetousness," "wrath," "strife," "emulation," "heresies," and such-like. Can it be possible, Pilgrim inquired, that the good Prince has left so dangerous a place as this without any safeguards or warnings?

No, said Experience. See, here is one posted right here, in plain sight: "What I say unto you I say unto all—watch;" and there, "Beware, lest ye also, being led away with the error of the wicked, fall from your steadfastness." (2 Pet. iii. 17.) It is not enough to start on a pilgrimage; the journey is beset with many dangers; and, without care, ten chances to one if we do not fail.

PILGRIM. I think, from these signs, we must be near the old road; the ground, also, seems firmer and dryer, and the storm-clouds are passing away. Indeed, the sun seems to shine clearer and nearer, seemingly, than ever. (Rom. viii. 28.) And, as if with a common impulse, they sung—

"God moves in a mysterious way,
His wonders to perform;
He plants his footsteps on the sea,
And rides upon the storm.

"You fearful saints, fresh courage take;
The clouds you so much dread
Are big with mercy, and shall break
In blessings on your head.

"Judge not the Lord by feeble sense,
But trust him for his grace;
Behind a frowning Providence
He hides a smiling face."

And as they sung, *Experience* lifted up his eyes, and with a joyful heart exclaimed, I see the Delectable Mountains. And sure enough, there they stood in the clear sunshine at some distance ahead of them. But on ascending an eminence to take a better view, they saw that the mountains were a long way off, although the road seemed quite plain. And as they looked along the highway that now lay so distinctly before them, who should they see walking on the road, arm and arm, but their dear brethren, *Faithful* and *Sincere*, from whom they had been separated in the storm. And so calling lustily to them, they succeeded in arresting their attention, when *Sincere*, turning, exclaimed, "Here are our dear brethren, *Pilgrim* and *Experience*, whom we had given up for lost: blessed be Immanuel, that the pit did not swallow them nor the storm destroy them. Let us wait till they come up."

So seeing them stop, *Pilgrim* and his companion quickened their pace and soon they were locked in each others' embrace. After mutual salutations and rejoicings were over, they related to each other their adventures in the valley.

After *Pilgrim* and *Experience* had finished, *Faithful* remarked: I find, after all, you did not suffer as I did. Soon after we began to run from the fiends I found myself in a by-path, as I judged to the left of the main road; but I was afraid to turn back, having lost sight of my Brother *Sincere*, and I feared to meet the enemy alone. And as my path seemed to incline again to the right, I kept on, in the hope of finding the highway again. The storm still continued, accompanied with thunder and lightning. As I went on, I perceived an opening a little way to the left hand, just before me, from whence seemed to proceed a faint light and strange noises. When I came opposite to it, I beheld a most petrifying sight. (Mar. iii. 29.) The mouth of the pit seemed to be open, and many were being dragged and thrown in, with the most heart-rending and dismal cries. (Jo. viii. 21.) I turned my eyes from it, stopped my ears, and was hastening away, when a fierce monster seized me. I struggled and broke from him, bidding him begone, for I was Immanuel's servant. He said he knew all that, but I was now upon his premises. These words weakened me much, so that I could not so well resist him. He then dragged me toward the pit. I struggled for help, and as he was hurrying me along, I caught at everything that might retard my progress. I perceived several low trees across the road where he dragged me, but I noticed the fiend endeavored to get me as far from these as he could so that I could not reach them. However, by a desperate struggle, I caught hold of a friendly branch of one of the trees that seemed to bend itself toward me. (Matt. viii. 25.) When the monster found I had got hold of it, he raged with hellish fury, and dragged me as if he would tear my arm from my body. But I twisted the pliant branch around my hand, and was determined to lose my arm or break the twig; but thanks to Immanuel, both resisted all his violence. When the tyrant had wasted his strength, he let me alone, saying, go your way. And as he left me, he threw something in my eyes, which so affected me that I thought that I was falling into the pit. But I kept hold of the tree till this passed away. My spirits then revived, and I made the best of my way back, still brandishing in my hand a branch of this tree which I had pulled off (Jo. xi. 26), lest I might be again attacked. Just then I heard a voice before me, and hastening up, to my inexpressible joy, found my good Brother *Sincere.*

SINCERE. As for me, I have fared but little better. I ran forward in the dark as fast I could through constant fear of stumbling, for the path was rough and difficult. The tempest roared among the trees and caverns of the valley. Hearing voices behind me, I turned and saw the same terrible troop near me; never did I before behold such a terrifying sight. I shut my eyes and kept on slowly and calmly as I could, ever feeling for the road, being determined to keep that; and although I heard horrid yells and blasphemies, yet I found that nothing dared to lay hold of me so long as I kept in the road. At length, observing that the fiends had no power to stop me, I cried out, "Though I walk through the valley and shadow of death, I will fear no evil for thou art with me; thy rod and thy staff comfort me." (Ps. xxiii. 4.) When lo! a voice came from over head, "For this purpose was the Son of God manifested that he might destroy the works of the Devil and deliver them who through fear of death, were all their lifetime subject to bondage." (1 Jo. iii. 8; Heb. ii. 15.) At this my spirits greatly revived, the weather cleared up and I came on, all the more joyful for my recent fear and trial. My joy was soon increased by finding my dear Brother *Faithful.* And now what pleasure on earth is so great as this sweet reunion? And lifting up their voices, they sung,

"We will not act the coward's part,
But onward all proceed;
Our captain shall his grace impart
In every time of need.
Great peace have they who love his cause
And on his word rely;
From such as keep his holy laws,
The enemy will fly.

"The world and sin may grieve us sore,
And rouse our weakest fears;
Our march is but a few days more,
Through this dark vale of tears.
Death may assail, and Satan too,
With his opposing powers,
But let us prove our valor true,
The victory is ours."

They had not gone far until they saw at a distance over to the right hand of the road, a person coming daintily along a beautiful path that crossed the road at an acute angle, and as he drew near *Faithful* hailed him, asking his name and destiny.

My name is *Probus*. I am going to the Celestial City, and so far I find it a pleasant journey. You look as though you had been out in a storm. I have heard of the dangers that beset the road you came, and I chose this more pleasant one, although it is a little further and seems to lay across yours.

SINCERE. But would not good company make amends for the rugged road, especially as you admit this road is straighter than the one you are on?

PROBUS. I am fond of company, and have no objection to accompany you, so long as something new and interesting may turn up; as to the distance, I am fond of rambling, especially where I can learn something, being naturally of an inquisitive turn.

PILGRIM. But how happened you to start for the Celestial City, and what do you expect to gain by going there?

PROBUS. In my researches I learned there probably was such a place, and I furthermore became satisfied that if the city where I lived were not destroyed, I could not always remain there. Then, also, the active mind loves a change; and having some leisure, I took it into my head to see if I could find the new city.

FAITHFUL. Pray from what town were you?

PROBUS. From the town of Self-Conceit, in the State of Carnal Security; my neighbors, generally, are not so inquisitive and stirring as I am, and, therefore, generally feel contented and satisfied with themselves.

PILGRIM. Had not the report reached your city that it was to be destroyed, and that all who did not repent were to perish miserably with it?

PROBUS. Oh, yes! yet, but few believed it, and those that did, felt as though we were safe, never having done anything wrong.

EXPERIENCE. Think you those on whom the tower in Siloam fell, and slew them (Luke xiii. 4), were sinners above all that dwelt in Jerusalem? I tell you nay, but except you repent you shall likewise perish. You do not seem to talk or act as though a sense of your danger, or the solemn and priceless interests at stake, rested upon you.

While thus conversing, they saw, at a distance, a

carriage waiting near a stile, which led into a beautiful field on the right side of the road. When they came near, they saw a sign over the stile with this inscription, "Field of Speculation." A beautiful path led through this field to another stile that came back again into the road. *Probus* at once recognized the carriage, and said it belonged to one *Clericus*, of the City of Orthodoxy. When *Pilgrim* started, saying, "Can it be that gentlemanly host that entertained us so pleasantly and showed us through the city?"

PROBUS. I presume it is the same. I know him well; he is a good, liberal-hearted fellow, of an inquisitive turn of mind, and I presume he has gone over here to make observations. The servant, who was with the carriage, told them that his master, on reading the inscription, had his curiosity excited, and had gone over the stile, telling him to wait his return, but that he had been gone so long he was uneasy about him.

Whereat, *Probus* looking over, and seeing a nice path, carpeted with beautiful flowers, made as though he would go over. *Sincere* remonstrated, telling him it was not safe to venture into new ways, as they were in a somewhat strange country, and he might get lost.

PROBUS. I am fond of adventure, and then this path seems well trodden, and comes again into the highway. I will go over, and if I find *Clericus*, I will bring him to the other end of the field, so you may drive the carriage to the other stile and wait there till we come.

Probus then went over and wandered in the Field of Speculation, leaving the rest to pursue their journey as they chose. He soon became so delighted with its beauties and fragrance that he could not confine himself to the path, ever thinking those flowers furthest from him were the most beautiful, so he hurried on to examine them, and stopped and turned so often to gaze and ponder, that the day wore off ere he was aware. The evening, however, was fine, and the soft moonbeams but gave a new turn to his observations, till, oppressed from excess of pleasure, he laid down under a beautiful hedge and spent the night in sweet dreams. He lay till the sun had risen, and was aroused by the melody of birds, when he rose and set out in search of *Clericus*. He wandered on till he came to the furthest side of the field, which he found enclosed with a high hedge, through which he peered and thought he discovered more beautiful flowers than any he had yet seen. This, he thought, was very fortunate, and if he could only get over, he would certainly have some new specimens to take back with him. After searching some time for an opening through the thicket, he saw a sign with this inscription, "Secret things belong to God." (Deut. xxix. 29.)

But, infatuated with the flowery prospect beyond, and filled with a desire to make some new discovery, he did not heed the admonition, but rashly went through. When he got in, he saw this inscription—

"Free Thinking." This, thought he, speaks well for the character of this field; so he wandered on, perfectly intoxicated in what he saw, nor did he think of food or rest until the sun went down, when he again fell asleep amidst the exquisite odors of countless flowers, while his very dreams continued the flowing imagery which filled his mind. And thus he lay till the sun was well on its journey, when, lo! he was roused by a huge giant, who, with a terrible voice and grim visage, demanded who he was, and what he was doing in his field.

PROBUS. I am but a pilgrim, going to the Celestial City.

GIANT. You may be a *pilgrim*, but this is not the way to *that* city, as I will soon convince you.

He then told Probus that he was on his ground, and was his property, and bade him get up and go with him. He then seized Probus, dragged him over the field of Free Thinking to a gloomy castle, situated in a thick wood. As they passed through the yard, Probus noticed groups of persons engaged in various diversions, perfectly indifferent to what was going on around them (Eph. v. 12), and, thrusting Probus into a dungeon, said:

GIANT. My name is Infidelity. You are now in the castle of Free Thinking. So you can go no further; and, if you content yourself, you shall fare as well and be as happy as those you saw at play in the court, and whom you may have noticed were blind; many of them were once as fond of rambling in search of future happiness as you, but have now concluded to eat and drink and be merry (Luke xii. 19), and let that end the matter.

Then was Probus in a sad mood, for he could not be satisfied to think this was to be the end of all man's hopes and desires.

The giant brought him food from the adjacent fields, but this only increased his misery, and he refused to eat. The giant told him he might as well eat and drink while he could, for he would soon die, and that would be the end. As to the Celestial City, and endless happiness, there was none. But, as Probus seemed obstinate, he seized him by the arm and led him through a dark hall, and, opening a rusty door at the further end, told him *that* was the Dungeon of Annihilation, and the only release he could promise was to thrust him in there. So, suiting the action to the word, he threw him in and bolted the terrible door. Poor Probus fell down astounded and horror-stricken. Alas! alas! exclaimed he, and can it be possible that all man's glowing hopes must end here? Are all the glorious visions concerning the future mere imagination? Is one single soul, capable of giving birth to thought, to be shut up in endless night? Is all religion founded in superstition? Are heaven, with all its glories, and hell, with all its fearful demands for justice, chimeras? I shudder at such horrid suggestions. How reason reels! If these things are so, its loins are unloosed; all is uncertainty, all is ruin! But, no, it is not so. I will not lay here! And shouting with energy, he heard a voice, saying, "The hour is coming when all that are in their graves shall come forth—they that have done good unto the resurrection of life, and they that have done evil to condemnation" (Jo. v. 29), and instantly the door flew open, and leaping up, Probus saw a stream of light, which he followed, and soon found himself ascending a flight of stairs to the top of the castle, when, to his surprise, he noticed a troop of soldiers approaching, brandishing in their hands the evidences of Christianity, headed by General Revelation, and his aid, Right Rules of Interpretation. Among the most active, he noticed Captain Reformer, whose batteries shook the castle to its foundation. Neither was the giant idle. He procured the forces of the rebel prince with whom he was in alliance, from the towns of Vanity, Sensuality, and Self-Conceit, and from the city of Destruction. The anxiety of Probus grew apace. At length he noticed, with joy, that a breach was made in the walls, through which he leaped, while the whole castle trembled as if it would fall down. He had scarcely gained the open field, when he saw Clericus emerging from another breach, which the giant also perceiving, aimed some of his most deadly shots at them, but all fell harmless as drops of rain.

Then falling prostrate on the ground, Clericus and Probus returned hearty thanks to Immanuel for their deliverance.

CLERICUS. But, friend Probus, how came you here? I was acquainted with your father's family, and slightly with you, but I never thought any of you had any inclination to go on a pilgrimage.

PROBUS. True, Mr. Clericus, but I became alarmed at the indifference of our whole city, and concluded I would like to see all there was to be seen in the broad world, and then go on to the Celestial City, of which I had heard so much. Seeing your carriage at the stile, I left the company of some excellent companions I fell in with on the road, and made a plea of searching for you, that I might gratify my curiosity to wander in these fields. But I became wise above what was written, have slighted good advice, and paid dear for my experience.

CLERICUS. And I, too, although my intentions were good, have carried my desire to gather up the good from all systems too far. The lesson we have learned may do us good. Let us now seek the old road (Jer. vi. 16), and strive, by our firmness, and courage, and perseverance, to induce as many as we can to walk in it; for we know, however rugged the path, or hard the trials, and great the dangers that may be found there, they are not to be compared with those found elsewhere. At this, they came to the stile, where they found the carriage of Clericus, with his faithful servant waiting; so, getting in, they directed him to keep the main road and make what speed he could, peradventure they might overtake the company, which the servant said had gone by some time before. They had not gone far before they descried, in the distance, a large town, called Merit, through which Clericus had formerly passed, and where he had found entertainment that used to suit him, the thought of which now was anything but agreeable. But, as they drew near and passed along, they descried a sign, with this inscription, "Pilgrim's Inn," on a new street, called Reformation street, where they stopped, and, to their joyful surprise, found the company of pilgrims for which they had been looking, who, in turn, were astonished and overjoyed to see Probus, whom they had given up for lost, and with him, their quondam friend, Clericus.

EXPERIENCE. Ah! my dear friend Probus, you have had a long ramble, and we feared you had met with some disaster. Let us hear the result of your adventure.

PROBUS. Pardon me, my brethren. We have thus far escaped, but are too tired to tell you all to-night; so, good landlord, let us have some refreshments, and, after a night's rest, we will gratify you.

CHAPTER XI.

CLERICUS AND PROBUS GIVE THEIR HISTORY—JOINED BY SIMPLE—DISCUSSION BY THE WAY—ARRIVE AT THE TOWN OF VANITY.

Ye therefore, beloved, seeing ye knew these things before, beware lest ye also, being led away with the error of the wicked, fall from your own steadfastness.—PET. iii. 17.

IN the morning *Probus* related what he had passed through, expressing his regret and sorrow for the sad experience, so that it drew tears of sympathy from every eye, while all expressed their preference for the right road, although it might lead through valleys, or over mountains strewed with flowers, or beset with thorns and thistles and tempests. If fiends and giants troubled them at times in the way, they troubled them worse out. If labors and trials, self-denials and sacrifices had to be endured to reach the city, 'twere better thus than fail of this and wander in blackness and darkness forever, and probably avoid some of these; so, dear *Probus*, said *Experience*, we hope to profit by your story.

PILGRIM. But, Brother *Clericus*, how is it that you are here? When and why did you leave the City of Orthodoxy? And how happened you to be caught in the castle?

CLERICUS. Your questions, my dear brother, though no doubt expressing your innocent anxiety to know, yet revives many painful reminiscences in my mind. I saw that the love of sect had grown into such a passion on the different streets, that it absorbed even their desire for the general welfare and the honor of the kingdom of the good Prince. I even became convinced of the truth of what that shrewd man, *Mr. Reformer*, said, that my labors at a world's convention of Christians would only result in a new party. I saw that the walls about the city were crumbling down, and in many places, as he said, you could not distinguish where it had been, and although each street was as strictly excluded from every other, as usual, yet the distinction between them and the world was growing fainter and fainter. I confess my mind was staggered. I grew nervous—sleep departed from me, and I concluded I would leave the city, at least for a season; and see if it would not benefit me, and through a secret inclining, I took the highway leading out toward the city of Refuge, thinking thereby I might see things that would please me better, and peradventure I might overtake you, for I was satisfied you would take the main road. So I drove on till I came to the hill, where you parted with *Formality*, and thinking the hill difficult and the road through the valley narrow, I took the road to the left, called the Way of the World. I saw *Formality* on the road; he said you had gone down into the valley, and probably that would be the end of you. The weather proved pleasant, and the roads good, so we made good speed, only stopping one night at Weathercock Inn, in the town of Civility. And as I came to the stile on the main road, back where you first saw my carriage, I was interested with the inscription I saw there, and so concluded at once, as I was out, rather on an excursion of observation, that I would go over into the field and spend a few hours; so bidding my servant tarry for me, I rambled on, readily found my way through into the field of Free Thinking, where I was suddenly and unexpectedly caught by the giant, and served in a similar way to *Probus*, only that, in consideration of my rank, I was allowed a pleasant room near the observatory, and saw the troop Brother *Probus* speaks of coming, and indeed felt satisfied they would succeed; and when I saw *Mr. Reformer* among them, I secretly rejoiced, although the *giant*, having flattered me a little, and pretended to place confidence in me, came and consulted me about the defense of the castle. I told him I had my fears. Just then the artillery thundered at the walls, and he left me. *Mr. Reformer*, noticing where I stood, and judging somewhat of my condition, directed a few solid shot, which struck the wall near where I stood, and instantly made a breach. I took advantage of the confusion, passed out, and deliberately walked off.

EXPERIENCE. Indeed, brethren, you may well be thankful to *Immanuel* for your deliverance, for it is not every one that escapes as well as you did. The good Prince has wisely set bounds to our speculative powers (Deut. xxix. 29), and it is neither safe or necessary to go beyond them—some become wise above what is written, and, too impatient to wait until they arrive at the Celestial City, turn aside into the field of Speculation; very soon they find themselves in the field of Free Thinking, are siezed by the Giant *Infidelity*, and borne away to his castle, mingle with the poor wretches you saw in the court, and give up their hopes in a future state for the vile short-lived pleasures of time.

CLERICUS. But how is it that so many fine, florid, intellectual-looking men are seen gathering about that castle yard?

EXPERIENCE. True, this is rather a queer, but important question. The rebel prince has obtained such a strange influence over the inhabitants of this province, and has so pampered their appetites and blinded their eyes, that they glory in their shame, and many of them never will see with an eye of faith, unless some sad affliction comes upon them. Their God is their stomach. (Phil. iii. 19.)

PROBUS. While I lay in the castle, I thought it was a pity we had not more, or clearer, evidence for a divine revelation.

EXPERIENCE. The difficulty, my brother, does not lie in the quantity nor brilliancy of the evidence, but in the pride and sensuality of poor, perverted human nature. When the appetite clamors, light becomes darkness, wisdom folly, reason—falsely so called—is deified, everything is perverted, and hence this is one of the strongest grounds for condemnation, that light has come into the world (Jo. i. 9); but men love darkness rather than light, because their deeds are evil. Hence the light shineth in darkness, and the darkness is too dense to receive it.

CLERICUS. As I lay there in the castle, I wondered how far curiosity and doubts and unbelief would carry a man.

EXPERIENCE. Only through this world. Devils are all believers. In hell there are no doubts. (Jas. ii. 19.) This, too, suggests the grand first principles of religion by which we must be guided through this world, namely, by faith in a divine code, confirmed by many incontrovertible and infallible witnesses—that is, witnesses having sound senses and judgment, and a perfect opportunity of knowing the things they give testimony of. To reject all these is rather proof of loss of reason, and seems to be a challenge to be given over to darkness of heart and reprobacy of mind; man is lost, bewildered, and when, in the pride of his own heart, he thinks to find his way, he is sure to go wrong; he finds he has not only no compass or pole-star, but no haven to steer to. Reason, when deducing its conclusion from the observations of the senses, stops with the grave, and, finding all dark beyond, writes over the gateway to the cemetery, "Death—an eternal sleep!" and thus makes man's wonderful gifts and aspirations abortive, gives the lie to *hope*, the noblest emotion of the soul, which

——Of all passions most befriends us here.
Passions of prouder name befriend us less
Joy has its sorrow, transport has its death;
Hope, like a cordial, innocent, though strong,
Man's heart at once inspires and serenes.

It cannot be that the Creator, who seems to have made man as the crown-piece of his works, should have given him such an impulse merely to make him more wretched. Hence, unless he be a strange exception, he must have an end proportioned to his aspirations and faculties.

All felt that these relations and discussions were profitable. But, as the day was advancing, Pilgrim proposed that they should at once proceed on their journey, as they were admonished that the journey was long and time precious; so, after a comfortable breakfast, they bade adieu to their kind landlord, when Clericus got into his carriage, taking Probus with him, and, promising to make arrangements for the rest at the next town, they departed.

Pilgrim, Faithful and Experience went on with light and cheerful hearts, inasmuch as they felt strengthened from what they had seen and heard, by the thought that the straightforward path of duty and right was safest and happiest. And as they journeyed onward, and were expressing their mutual pleasure and determination, they saw a man coming along a path that seemed to enter the highway just ahead of them. The man seemed to be absorbed in thought, and somewhat excited. Whereupon, Faithful hailed him.

FAITHFUL. You seem, sir, to be somewhat troubled. May I inquire where you are from, and the cause of your trouble?

SIMPLE. My name is Simple. I am from Filthy Lucre street, in the town of Vanity, not far ahead of you. We had just opened a mine in our neighborhood that bid fair to yield richly of gold and silver, together with several other precious metals, and things seemed to be moving on finely. A market had been opened over in Avarice avenue, in the same city, in which flesh and bones and souls of men and women were the chief articles of merchandize, which, although it did not prove a source of much gain, yet it so ministered to the ease, and so pampered the pride and passions of the inhabitants of that avenue, that they felt as though all others were born merely to administer to their comfort—that even the laws should be so changed that their wicked traffic would be legalized and the reins of government put into their own hands.

FAITHFUL. But was not their business lawful when they began? And how happens it that this should trouble you?

SIMPLE. Well, when the laws of the city were first made, for the sake of peace the people agreed that they might continue it, because they felt that they were too weak to banish it at once from the city. But the mistake soon grew apparent: constant trouble arose between these human merchants and the police of the city, until now there is a civil war between them, and that of a more serious character than any anticipated; and it threatens to involve, and seriously to affect, the whole city; and although we live in one of the most out-of-the-way streets, yet we feel greatly alarmed, and I was just pondering upon these things when I met you.

FAITHFUL. But your city has a fame for being enlightened, has it not? Certainly, they will compromise this matter?

SIMPLE. Yes, sir, but fame is not always just; 'tis sometimes like an old sign that remains on a building when all the contents and use of the house are changed; or, like the whited sepulchres, beautiful without, within full of dead men's bones. So it is in this case; for this struggle has already developed, by deeds of atrocity and acts of treachery, a state of degradation and barbarism that throws into the shade the blackest corner of savage life. And as to compromise, these things being so, they that have brought on this trouble neither desire nor will allow, while the good of humanity and the anger of a Holy God alike forbid it. (Isa. xix. 1.) Moral corruption has been so long accumulating in the city, that, like a ripened boil, it must come out, core and all, before the body can get well.

FAITHFUL. Are there not Christians all through your city, and will they not act as salt to prevent this trouble from going to so serious a length as you apprehend? Certainly they will be on the side of law and order, especially when wickedness stirs up the trouble. Will they not be a unit in efforts to remove the cause, maintain the government, and prevent barbarians from overrunning that city?

SIMPLE. Well, as to that, I am not so certain. I take it that Christians are men still liable to the weaknesses common to humanity; and that strange traffic, which, as I said, gave rise to our troubles, seems to have affected the very atmosphere they breathe. Among the purchases are luxuries and ease, freedom from labor, and a chance to exercise petty authority, which is so congenial to poor human nature, that it at once turns to *tyranny*, and this blunts the feelings, blinds the eyes, and turns the head and heart both. Hence, so far from being a unit to remove the cause, maintain the government, and prevent *fratricidal* trouble, not only professors of religion, but preachers of talent and standing, have taken up on the side of the cruel and relentless mob. Some have fallen with hearts swollen with rage, their hands dripping with fratricidal blood, and their souls spotted all over with treason, rushing into the presence of their God, who said, "they shall receive unto themselves damnation;" others still live to urge on these murderous bands or plead their cause.

PILGRIM. Brethren, these things are strange and startling to me. Little did I think, when I started on a pilgrimage, that I should hear such things. Can nothing be done to restore order in the city whence Mr. Simple came? Certainly, if we are to pass through that city, our own safety is involved; and then, how can we see others suffering and not try to help them?

EXPERIENCE. Most assuredly, although our company is small, yet, if we act prudently, we may do the more good thereby, since they will respect us for our *goodness* more than our *power*, feel the weight of our piety and self-denying example when they see that it is free from intrigue, and be inclined to follow our counsel when we show them that it has in view only the greatest good of all. The good Prince designed we should act as the light of the world and salt of the earth, by mingling with them, and letting our light be seen and our influence felt; and, while we give every encouragement to the powers that be, who are striving to preserve order and discourage by every means those who have thus risen up against the peace of the city, we must set earnestly to work purifying the fountains, administering the bread and water of life to the famishing, and applying the leaves of the tree of life to the suffering.

FAITHFUL. But is it right for us to have anything to do with this trouble? Does it not belong to politicians, and are we not, as pilgrims, bound just to keep right on our journey and attend to our legitimate business?

EXPERIENCE. This is our legitimate business, as I have before said. Now, if the salt loses its savor, all is lost. This state of things was brought about by pursuing the course specified. Religion and politics cannot be separated, because the same person is interested in both. Man, however soundly regenerated and pure, is involved in all the true interests of time until he passes into eternity. Hence, God designed rulers to be men fearing God—not ruling by virtue of religious office or standing, but being pure, God-fearing, they will administer the affairs of state with an eye single to God's glory, and then all can lead quiet and peaceable lives in godliness and honesty. But this making political character and duties so separate and different, has induced a feeling that they must be different, till there is no more striking contrast than politician and Christian. And the world has ever found that when the wicked rule the people mourn. God has connected every effect with a legitimate cause, nor should we expect any end without making use of the proper means.

FAITHFUL. Do I understand you, Brother Experience, that political rulers should be good men, Christians, and that Christians should mingle in these strifes, and that Christians are responsible for the preservation of order in the world?

Experience. As to mingling in strife, if you mean this in a malicious sense, I think not. All God ordains is right. If the powers that be are ordained of God, its agents should be ministers of God in deed, God-fearing and God-honoring men. If God wills to repay vengeance on evil doers, the instrument he uses cannot be guilty for so acting. Paul says, "The saints shall judge the world" (1 Cor. vi. 2); that is, good, pious men must rule, before millennial order can be restored. The decree has gone forth, wicked men and short-sighted professors have stood in the way; but now I believe the troubles Simple speaks of to be the beginning of the breaking up of the foundation that we may build aright. And if ever the church was called upon to work, this is the time. The Gospel should be brought to bear upon the heart as the power of God unto salvation—schools established for all, and especially the incredible masses that have been kept in utter ignorance by this inhuman traffic, *Simple* speaks of. Piety must take possession of legislators' hearts, and goodness nerve the arms of the executive. God now holds the church responsible for this great work. He is opening the way, and says, "Enter and occupy."

By this time the day was well nigh spent, and the pilgrims found themselves drawing near to a fine-appearing, popular, busy town, which *Simple* told them was called the town of Vanity; and, although it was filled with vain people, who thought more of the present than the future, and abounded with trinkets, and things to please the fancy; and although without constant watchfulness, they would be led into some sinful trap, yet there were some good people there, and a few houses had been opened of late, where pilgrims would find a welcome, pleasant, and safe home.

As they passed along the streets, they were struck with the stately and gaudy appearance of some of the largest buildings. These *Sincere* told them, to their surprise, were churches, devoted to the worship of the humble Nazarene. As they gazed at their lofty pinnacles, stained windows, and chimes of bells, the gorgeous pulpits, cushioned seats, and sonorous organs, they wondered whether this amazing display of wealth had left a single dark, heathen, or poverty-stricken corner of the earth unsupplied with the Gospel. Just here, their attention was drawn to a man standing in the door of a plain, but neat and commodious building, beckoning them in; so, on drawing near, they were joyfully surprised to find *Clericus*, who welcomed them in the name of the master of the house, who, although absent for a little while, had made every arrangement for their comfort, and wished them to feel themselves at home.

CHAPTER XII.

MEETING IN THE TOWN OF VANITY—REFORMERS REFORMING—ALL FEEL BENEFITED AND GO FORTH TO LABOR WITH RENEWED ZEAL—LEVELING, YET ELEVATING, AIM OF THE GOSPEL.

Therefore seeing that we have this ministry, as we have received mercy we faint not. But have renounced the hidden things of dishonesty, not walking in craftiness nor handling the word of God deceitfully; but by mainfestations of the truth, commending ourselves to every man's conscience in the sight of God.—2 COR. iv. 1, 2.

THIS was as joyful as it was unexpected, nor had they been here long before many brethren began to assemble from various parts of the country, and notwithstanding the terrible commotion, beginning in Avarice avenue, and spreading to other streets, it soon proved to be one of the largest meetings of its kind. The brethren assembled with a vague feeling that it was a meeting involving most important interests and consequences. The foundations of society were giving way. The fallow ground was broken up. Evidently a new state of things was about to be introduced. And at such times, nothing is of more importance than that the *religious* element receive a proper direction, since upon this the *shaping* and *destiny* of society depends. The venerable *Reformer* was present, and, although somewhat superannuated, yet his presence added much weight to the meeting, and his eloquent address, as President of the meeting, was filled with sublime thoughts and matured counsels, and was looked upon by his younger brethren as among his last efforts.

The addresses made by others, too, showed that his mantle had fallen largely upon many *Elishas;* and the interest of the meeting became intense. Few homes or hearts remained untouched by the thrilling scenes and bloody fruits of the pending struggle. To be indifferent, or neutral, was sinful, because in all such cases this was to encourage or favor the wrong; as the good Prince had said: "He that is not for me is against me." (Luke xi. 23). And "he that gathereth not with me scattereth abroad." Hence this seemed to be the time when the influence of this great Reformation was to be cast on the side of order, justice, and progress, or against it. While the Secretary's report showed that the great work of imbuing the minds of the world, with the principles of the *Restoration* of the Bible teaching in its purity, had made great progress, yet the reports of different committees showed an enlarged and liberal zeal in pushing the work forward.

But the crisis was approaching when the meeting was to be called upon, as the representative of a great people, to range itself upon one side or the other of the great struggle pending—a struggle which involved great principles of justice and human progress. And when it came, notwithstanding a few hung back, yet the mass promptly and earnestly stepped out upon the side of law and progress in the direction they had been travelling. The embodied spirit of the meeting was clear and firm. And as it drew to a close the pathetic exhortations and touching counsels of the venerable *veterans* in this great work seemed to give an increased zeal to all, and with renewed covenants they went forth to labor in the great vineyard.

Even *Clericus* had received new views and felt a new impulse, and henceforth determined to gird himself and journey with his brethren, believing that the life-struggle had assumed new and more earnest shapes.

They had not gone far ere *Probus* began:—Brethren, you all, no doubt, had your impressions during the meeting and have drawn your own conclusions; but I must confess some things are very strange to me and difficult to reconcile with the spirit and design of the Gospel. Certainly I cannot be mistaken in this, that "spiritual and eternal things are of greatest value" (Matt. vi. 33), and hence should absorb every other; that all political, temporal things are secondary, and should be held in abeyance.

FAITHFUL. True, dear *Probus*, but our *earthly* side is very sensitive, and because brethren differ, and sometimes pull apart, it only shows the obstinacy of human nature in its corrupt form, and the difficulty of keeping the body under. (1 Cor. ix. 27.) And even two apostles separated with contention (Acts xv. 39) because of much less matters than those that have disturbed the peace of some brethren to-day.

The Gospel was intended to elevate the affections

disenthral humanity, and redeem the soul; but it does not wholly destroy the emotions of the flesh.

CLERICUS. A very good distinction, truly, it *overcomes.* But early education and prejudice in a thousand lurking forms rise, like strong men armed to resist, clouds and storms arise from the earthly side; but the sunshine of faith will break through these, and the day will be clear.

EXPERIENCE. My good *Clericus,* you speak my mind also. But I tremble at the insights I sometimes get of the condition of humanity and the workings of Divine Providence. Man without *Free Agency* could not be man, and, although, *this* may suffer the *individual* to come wide of *the mark,* yet Providence will encompass *the end.*

PILGRIM. I well remember the *paintings* I saw when on a visit to *Mr. Interpreter* with *Evangelist.* That *vision* has been before my mind ever since, and I confess it has awakened in me a curiosity upon some points not yet fully gratified. And your speaking of *the end* revives it. What is *the end* of all *this?* And why is the *rebel prince* allowed to hold such sway, leading the greatest majority into *rebellion?* Can it be the *design* of the Creator that there should be more *sin* and *suffering* than joy?

CLERICUS. Suffer me to hint, my brethren, that there are many things mysterious to us because of our limited understandings, which, to an All-seeing eye, may be perfectly consistent. One thing is clear—that the *Revealed Law* of God, by which sin alone is determined, brings great happiness when obeyed; and when disobeyed misery follows. The wise Solomon seems to have argued and settled the whole question as follows: "Let us hear the conclusion of the whole matter; fear God, and keep his commandments, for this is the whole happiness of man." If, then, this is the *end* of God's commandments, was it not his *design* in creation?

EXPERIENCE. Truly so; and as to there being more sin and suffering than joy, I think this is also doubtful. It is not an enlightened or liberal view that claims this little earth of ours as the whole of the Creator's dominion; and yet several passages of Scripture seem to indicate that Satan's work was confined to *this earth.* He "was cast out into the earth," and called "the prince of this world." *Here* he seems to have dominion, and to work ruin, present and everlasting.

PILGRIM. How fearful, then, is the experiment of humanity—

"I tremble at myself,
And in myself am lost.
Oh! what a miracle to man is man."

And yet I now begin to see and understand what *Mr. Evangelist* told me about the *good Prince* and the *rebel prince.* A great struggle going on for a time, and the *good Prince* finally coming and destroying or burning up the city of the *rebel prince,* or this world. And also of reading in this volume of reports (2 Pet. iii. 7) that "the heavens and earth are . . . reserved unto fire against the day of judgment and perdition of

13

ungodly men." And all this but increases my desire to prosecute my pilgrimage.

PROBUS. Yes, Brother Pilgrim, you express my feelings also. I trust, and indeed feel assured, that "all things will work together for good." That men will be led to see things in their true light. That high places will be made low, the rough places smooth, and the crooked ways straight, and the blessed Gospel of the grace of God triumph over all human passions and errors, redeeming and elevating and blessing the whole race of mankind; when

"The brute-hearted temper of man shall grow tame,
The wolf and the lion lie down with the lamb,
The bear with the kine shall contentedly feed,
And children their young ones in harmony lead.

"No more shall the sound of the war-whoop be heard,
The ambush and slaughter no longer be feared;
The tomahawk, buried, shall rest in the ground,
And peace and good-will to the nations abound.

"Roll forward, blest Saviour, roll forward the day
When all shall submit and rejoice in thy sway;
When men of all nations, united in praise,
One vast hallelujah triumphant shall raise."

Thus musing, they found the time rapidly gliding; and, in the glittering beauty of the setting sun, they saw the spires and windows of a little village, whither they bent their steps in hopes of entertainment, and were not disappointed.

CHAPTER XIII.

ARRIVAL AT THE TOWN OF BEREA—USE AND DANGER OF VARIOUS ROADS—PILGRIMS MAKE PROGRESS—GLIMPSE OF THE CELESTIAL CITY.

While we look not at the things which are seen, but at the things which are not seen, for the things which are seen are temporal, but the things which are not seen are eternal.—2 COR. iv. 18.

ON arriving at the village before them, they saw many unostentatious but commodious buildings, and seeing the multitude thronging toward one with books in their hands, they joined in, and to their joyful surprise on entering they saw the love beaming countenance of *Evangelist*, surrounded by the people who sat with open books, listening and asking questions. (Acts xvii. 11.) And such interest and delight did he take in his work, that at first he did not notice the pilgrims. But even this afforded them exquisite pleasure, while they sat obscurely drinking in the sweet influences of a genial atmosphere, looking at the home-like surroundings, and listening to the earnest, plain, soul-cheering lessons they drew from the blessed book, and anticipating the brotherly recognitions and reunions they knew would follow the close of the lesson, when they should be recognized. But *Mr. Evangelist* waxed warm as he talked of the approaching fate of the city of *Destruction*, the kindness of the good *Prince*, in preparing a city of

Refuge. "And now," said *Evangelist*, "to you is the word of this salvation sent. He that believeth and is baptised shall be saved, and he that does not shall be damned. Make no vain excuses. Think not to say in your hearts, who shall ascend up into heaven, to bring Christ down from above, or who shall descend into the deep, that is to bring him up again from the dead; or, to demand some other work or way, for the directions are before you, in the words of this Holy Book, to be believed. And now, if you will believe on the good Prince, harden not your hearts by delay, tempt him not by asking more; arise, and be baptised and wash away your sins, calling on the name of the Lord.

"Weeping sinners, dry your tears,
Jesus on the throne appears,
Mercy comes with balmy wing,
Bids you his salvation sing.

"Peace he brings you by his death,
Peace he speaks with ev'ry breath,
Can you slight such heavenly charms,
Flee! O, flee! to Jesus' arms."

The conviction was deep, the feeling intense, tears flowed freely, and as he closed, by saying, "Whosoever *will*, let him take the waters of life freely." Many men and women rushed forward, and confessed that "they did believe with all their hearts, that Jesus was the Christ, the Son of God." Then said,

EVANGELIST. Who can forbid water that these should not be baptised. And straightway he commanded them to be baptised in the name of the Lord Jesus, in order that they might receive remission of their sins, the gift of the Holy Spirit, and an inheritance among those who are sanctified by faith.

How clear was duty, how scriptural these ideas, how joyful this hour. *Clericus* could not contain himself, but burst out in tears and exhortations.

CLERICUS.

> "This is the way I long have sought,
> And mourned because I found it not."

Brethren, I scarcely know at which I am most joyful. The superabounding grace of *Immanuel*, in making this way so plain, or at seeing so many yield to the sweet influences of this occasion. Happy are you whose ears hear and whose hearts believe, and who are thus induced to flee for refuge and lay hold on the hope set before you. And with many other words did he testify, saying, "save yourself from this untoward generation."

After the meeting it was difficult to tell which were filled most with pleasure, the throbbing hearts of the pilgrims at finding themselves in so congenial a place, or the beaming countenance of *Evangelist* at their unexpected presence.

After the most cordial greetings and welcomes, *Evangelist* inquired, My brethren, what speed have you been making, how passed you the many dangers, and how endured you the many trials of the country through which you passed?

PILGRIM. My good brother, truly, the Lord has been gracious to us, and he has been with us, else we should have been destroyed, had it not been for the clear counsels given by *Mr. Interpreter*, at the house *Beautiful.* For truly, have we heard many "lo! here's, and lo! there's," and seen many cross roads and by-paths, and many apparently respectable people walking in them. Still from the *rules* given, we have been able to find *Immanuel's path*, which has led us hither.

SINCERE. Yes, and deeply has it been pressed upon my mind, from various reckonings and signs in this place and atmosphere, that we cannot be far from those *Delectable Mountains*, a glimpse of which we had from the *observatory* on the *house Beautiful.*

EVANGELIST. You judge truly, my brother, after passing a valley or two, where there are some peculiar dangers, known only when you get into them, but which you may pass in safety, if you "give heed to the sure word of prophecy" (2 Pet. i. 19), and be not deceived by outward appearances.

FAITHFUL. But may I inquire the name of this delightful little village, that seems so cheerful?

EVANGELIST. *Berea;* and it is noted for the salubrity of its climate, the intelligence and hospitality of its inhabitants: therefore do pilgrims delight to take it in their way to the *city of Refuge.* Here you will find such repose and fare as is delightful and strengthening for your journey. Hard by runs a beautiful river (Jo. iv. 14), whose waters will greatly refresh you, and upon its banks grow trees whose precious fruit will restore the wear and tear of the toil and care (Rev. xxii. 2) of your journey. Indeed, this beautiful river winds along your road till the end of your journey; and then, indeed, you will find its source bubbling up in the very city of God. So right welcome are you, my brethren; make yourselves entirely at home (Heb. xiii. 2), and, after a season of refreshment, you will be better prepared for your journey. The brethren delight to entertain you.

Then, being introduced to the brethren, they received many cordial invitations to partake of their hospitality. And truly were they in good case, insomuch that *Clericus* was as one bewildered.

CLERICUS. Truly, my brethren, this seems like belonging to the same family. (Matt. xxiii. 8.) How unlike the cold formality of my native city! There it was quite improper to be familiar and free. On casual visits each one was expected to go to the hotel, and at meetings it was considered rude to presume upon the inability of any one to provide themselves a home so far as to invite them to the uncertainties of the domestic circle.

The meeting waxed in interest, and this weary band felt well paid for their brief sojourn. Among the many precious entertainments afforded them was another view of the *Delectable Mountains*, which seemed very near; also, a glimpse of the *Celestial City*, that seemed to be basking in a clearer sunshine just beyond, and made them long to be on their journey, although they saw the smoke and mist that hung upon the valleys alluded to by *Evangelist*. So, being strengthened by many exhortations and good counsel from *Evangelist*, they went on their way.

Now it came to pass, as they journeyed onward in sweet conversation about the things pertaining to the *Celestial City*, they noticed a perceptible improvement in the whole country. The atmosphere seemed more salubrious, and their senses seemed dancing with delight under some strange influence that seemed to pervade all the air, when *Probus*, ever on the alert, looking a little to the right, saw, not far away, a beautiful orchard, which, as they drew near, proved to be in full bloom; and the odors from their sweet-scented blossoms at once accounted for the delightful emotions they had been the subjects of. The whole country was beautifully undulating and variegated: here were beautiful groves, and vineyards too, interspersed with bubbling fountains, while the sweet warbling of feathered songsters filled all the air—when, all at once, *Pilgrim* bethought him of the view given them by *Interpreter* from the observatory of the house *Beautiful* (Jo. xvii. 17), and assured them they should find it along this road. And, said

PILGRIM. My brethren, all these things make me certain this is *Immanuel's* land. Certainly the lines have fallen unto us in pleasant places. (Psa. xvi. 6.) We have a goodly heritage. And so they went on, singing,

"When verdure clothes the fertile vale,
And blossoms deck the spray,
And fragrance breathes in every gale,
How sweet the vernal day!

"Hark! how the feathered warblers sing!
'Tis Nature's cheerful voice;
Soft music hails the lovely spring,
And woods and fields rejoice.

"Oh! God of nature and of grace,
Thy heavenly gifts impart;
Then shall my meditation trace
Spring blooming in my heart.

"Inspired to praise, I then shall join
Glad nature's cheerful song;
And love and gratitude divine
Attune my joyful tongue."

CHAPTER XIV.

TEMPORAL THINGS CHANGE—THOSE GOVERNED BY THEM IN DANGER—DELECTABLE MOUNTAINS—(A WELL-ORDERED CHURCH)—THE IMPORTANCE OF A SCRIPTURAL ASSURANCE.

But I keep under my body, and bring it into subjection, lest that by any means, when I have preached to others, I myself should be a castaway.—1 Cor. ix. 27.

It is not for sunshine and flowers always to continue unchanged in an atmosphere so subject to storms and clouds and revolving seasons. Nay, rather should these blossoms fall to make way for fruit, and showers succeed to sunshine, and autumn to summer, that the fruit may be ripened and fitted for the garner. To sift *faith* from *feeling*, then, and the *promises* and *assurances* of the Gospel from the vascillating *emotions* of *our own hearts,* is the lifelong duty of the pious pilgrim, lest the adversary lead us to confound them, and so obtain an advantage, making us believe, when all goes well, God is very gracious to us, and, when storms arise, that his Spirit be taken from us. Pure streams and silver lakes give freshness, health, and life through all the air, while death-laden miasms exhale from stagnant pools and sluggish marshes. So is it in society. We feel revived by the very atmosphere of a living church. Where the Spirit of the Lord is, there is liberty; and we can but feel it, and, energised by it, we are strong, active, and happy. But when this salt loses its savor, corruption ensues: when this light becomes darkness, how great is that darkness!

Thus soliloquized *Clericus* as they journeyed on. Truly, my brethren, said he, that was a precious interview.

"My soul would always dwell
In such a frame as this,
And sit and sing itself away
To everlasting bliss."

But then the Master appoints these refreshing seasons (Heb. x. 25) to prepare us for the stern life-struggles before us. He designed that pilgrims should mingle with the world in person, while separated in character. Among the fruits we bear, "that others, seeing our good works, should be led to glorify our Father in Heaven."

RESOLUTE. I feel much of all that Brother *Cleri-*

cus has expressed, and I have thought the warnings so often given were made necessary by the presence of dangers along our journey, and the weakness of our natures.

> "We should suspect some danger nigh
> Where we possess delight,"

seems to be in keeping with the rule, "What I say unto you I say unto all—watch." (Mark xiii. 37.) But, certainly, one would think in such a beautiful country as this there cannot be many dangers, and these extensive orchards, with their abundant promise, seem to provide against future want.

SINCERE. True, my dear brother; what you have said is most true, and may be very useful. Let us not forget it; and I have been wondering if what Brother *Evangelist* said about appearances could refer to these beautiful circumstances.

PILGRIM. But see, my brethren, yonder is that beautiful river Brother *Evangelist* told us of. I had almost forgotten it and the distance we had travelled over during our conversations, and wrapped in such pleasing thoughts. I notice, too, the road begins to descend into a valley just ahead of us; so let us go and quench our thirst from the river, and rest us a while ere we enter the valley. And, as they did so, with one voice they sang—

> "What though the desert's heat annoy,
> These waters still renew our joy;
> And, while we drink this cheering spring,
> Upon its banks we sit and sing.

"While through life's barren waste we stray
This stream shall follow all the way;
Best flowers shall spring where'er it flows,
And deserts blossom as the rose!"

Then, as they went on, and drew near the valley to go down into it, they noticed that the road seemed slightly to incline to the left, the appearance of the country rapidly changed, and irregular hills arose on either hand. So, while they were remarking these things, *Pilgrim* espied, on the road ahead of them, a group of men, that seemed to be going the same way; so, quickening their pace, they soon came up with them, and found them to be *Mr. Trim*, *By-ends*, and *Pliable*.

RESOLUTE. Good day, gentlemen. You seem to be journeying in the same direction. May I inquire whither you are bound?

PLIABLE. We are on our way to the *Celestial City*, and shall be glad of your company.

BY-ENDS. And may one be so bold as to inquire where you are going? for I take it from your appearance you are travellers.

RESOLUTE. We are pilgrims from the city of Destruction to the city of Refuge, and would be glad to receive or communicate any intelligence or encouragement concerning the journey.

TRIM. True. This betokens a right spirit, and very much of your safety will depend in not meddling with the manners and customs of the inhabitants along the road, since all are very sensitive on these points.

RESOLUTE. Well, sir, had we received this caution before we came to *Berea,* or to those beautiful orchards, or the fruitful country through which we have passed, it might not seem so strange; but just now, on entering this gloomy, barren valley, it strikes me as strange.

TRIM. I was not aware, sir, that the places you mention were any more fruitful than this, or the country beyond. You will, I think, sir, find a great deal of refinement and good sense among the citizens. I have lived in this region myself for many years; and although I must confess we have had many struggles with improprieties and innovations, yet we have made out to live here, built a very nice church, which you may have noticed soon after you entered the valley, and are getting things in very nice order.

RESOLUTE. I have seen nice order in a graveyard, but it was the order of death. But, pray, what do you mean by improprieties and innovations?

PLIABLE. If one may presume to speak for a modest man, as Brother *Trim* is, I will answer. The training of society is a very responsible matter, and when he came among us there was much confusion. Some said one thing and some another, which was not very edifying. Some wanted one thing and some another. But Brother *Trim* took the helm, and, having a superior taste, just interposed his *authority,* and soon brought order out of chaos.

SINCERE. I remember seeing the church, as we passed, but I noticed the path did not seem much beaten about it—things seemed nice and clean, however. Is your church well attended? Are you bearing much fruit, by way of having additions to your church, and lively meetings?

PLIABLE. Very true, things seem quiet. We do not use any worldly and wicked means to excite and draw out the people, such as having instrumental music, or inflammatory, political speeches in the pulpit, and hence the curious don't come to our meetings, and, in fact, many of our giddy members are going elsewhere. But then, what Brother *Trim* does, he does right. None but the most proper and Gospel discourses in the pulpit, precise and masculine prayers and exhortations in the social meeting; and, hence, although our meetings are not lively, and numbers rather falling off, yet we have the exquisite pleasure of knowing that we carry out the Scripture and act from principle.

CLERICUS. Ah! friend, the heart is deceitful, and especially with the self-conceited; everything seems to be from *principle* that they do, and the *Scripture* must be very stiff, that *they* cannot bend to their aid. I know full well what all this means, and as I now look back to the city of *Orthodoxy* where I was reared, and see an *altar* reared to every *notion* and *ordinance* of man's invention, I feel a strong surprise at the exquisite pleasure we all felt, that we acted from *principle*, and were sustained by Scripture. But having, as I trust, got my eyes open, I scarcely know at which to wonder most, man's duplicity or the plainness of the Scripture.

TRIM. But, sir, do you mean to say, that the

Scripture authorizes a licentious freedom, that would make the house of God a *Babel,* or a *play-house,* where strains of music should cater to carnal fancy, and every one should have something to say, whether it would edify or not?

CLERICUS. I mean to say, that the Spirit of the Gospel is one of liberality, and humility, and zeal, that, while it would shun sin, yet seeks the sinner. Paul says, "He became all things to all men, that he might by all (innocent) means save some." (1 Cor. ix. 22.) True, we should not be reckless of means, but when the house is on fire, and the inmates asleep, or so absolved in play, that they either know or heed it not, we forget our precise formality, and shout and struggle to arouse and get them out. As to edifications, nothing so administers to this, as to cultivate a feeling of equality and earnest piety and zeal. Edification lays not in rhetoric so much as the lispings of love and piety.

TRIM. But, sir, I positively object to allowing anything the apostles did not allow. They taught the church to be subject to the Elders, who were to *rule* with *all authority.* Did not we labor hard and prayerfully to build up the churches and restore the ancient manners? Neither shall this ground be given up without a struggle. Whoever heard of the stupid and grovelling practice of *choir* and *instrumental music* in the church in the days of Peter, and did not Paul absolutely forbid *women* to open their mouths in the church?

RESOLUTE. Brethren, it has occurred to me, while

listening to this discussion, that much depends upon the temperament of the interpreter, as to what the apostles intended. Evidently, Brother *Trim* does not demand that we should confine ourselves to the same means only that the apostles used, and go on foot, while the world and Satan used the *press*, and go by *railroad* and *steam*, to sow the seeds of vice and false philosophy, and knowing full well the power of music, make use of it in every place where men need *inspiring* as well as pleasing. Whoever heard of Paul or Peter preaching in a pulpit, or putting cushions in the seats and carpets on the floors, of using a baptistry or burning gas, and yet I hear all these are in your church; and, indeed, I heard that Brother *Trim* published a religious newspaper, and travelled in the cars to spread the old Jerusalem Gospel, and was highly entertained by most excellent brethren and sisters, whose parlors were provided with the finest carpets, ornamented with marble mantels, loaded with tasteful vases, and with instruments of music, from which their sons and daughters discoursed sweet music, that greatly refreshed his weary frame.

PLIABLE. Ah! yes, Brother *Resolute*, we may innocently indulge in these things at home, but then to think of desecrating the house of God with musical instruments! This is horrible! Why there are many old brethren and sisters that would quit going to meeting if an instrument of music were to be introduced there. Better drive the young all away to other places where they can find music to their taste, if they all go to hell through orthodox churches, under orthodox music. Music never converted anybody, unless it was to fashionable flummery, called religion.

PROBUS. I see, Brother Pliable, you are willing that every erroneous and wicked cause may use enticements, but none should be *enticed* where they will hear the Gospel and so be saved.

TRIM. Shall we do evil that good may come? You acknowledge that music is merely enticing, gratifying to the fancy, and therefore, must be sinful.

PROBUS. I do not acknowledge that music is merely enticing, it is this, but it is more, it is edifying, entrancing, and you are to prove that *instruments* are in themselves sinful, or the music made upon them. David, the man after God's own heart, when in his most pious frame, used the *harp*, to accompany and elevate the strains of his praise. (Ps. cxlix. 3; cl. 3, 4.) And the wisest and greatest preacher the world ever saw, had the finest choir (Eccl. ii. 8), and had with it the greatest variety of musical instruments, all of which appears to have been acceptable to God. And, finally, the last most wonderous *choir*, that combined the diapason of the redeemed from the whole earth, had "every one of them harps" (Rev. v. 8), and with them they sung that wonderous song, expressive of the gratitude of the redeemed out of every nation under the whole heavens. I wonder how those old brethren and sisters that indulge in such a holy hatred of musical instruments on earth, would feel if they were present when this song was sung.

TRIM. I consider the young upstart, sir, that would speak disrespectfully of these dear old brethren and sisters deserves rebuking, and while I have a tongue and pen, their worldly-minded, pleasure-seeking plans shall be rebuked.

RESOLUTE. And know you, sir, that rebukes and rebuker, like the unbelieving lord in the days of Ahab (2 Kings vii. 17), shall be overborne by the onward march of the true spirit of the Gospel, freedom and conquest. These rebukes will as certainly fail you, as your Scripture authority, of which you have none. I know such a spirit commonly supplies the place of Scripture argument, but its result will leave your seats vacant and greatly lessen the number of the redeemed.

PILGRIM. Brethren, being somewhat anxious about our whereabouts, as I find we have passed over a large space since this interesting discussion began, I have been examining my pocket-compass, and I find that this road we are now upon, verges too much to the left, and as I noticed a path just ahead that turned more to the right, and seemed to ascend the hill, I thought I would call your attention to it.

BY-ENDS. This road, sir, keeps along in the valley, the scene of Brother *Trim's* labors, and I will assure you, you will find a pleasant route to the *city*.

CLERICUS. Yes, my brethren, I think we had better take the road indicated by Brother *Pilgrim*, for the atmosphere of this valley seems oppressive, the water is not good, the streams are drying up, there are no flowers, and the fruit is scarce and poor.

And as if by a common impulse, they turned to the right, and began to ascend the hill, while *Trim*, *Pliable* and *By-ends* quickening their pace, soon disappeared down the valley, so they went on, being surprised as they ascended to find groves and vineyards and orchards, similar to those they had recently passed, and soon discovered the secret in finding their path verged toward the beautiful river, along whose banks they had previously wandered, and from whose waters they had been so refreshed, and they saw just before them the Delectable Mountains.

As they ascended to the tops of the mountains, they found shepherds feeding their flocks among the orchards and vineyards. And although they seemed at once, from everything they saw around them, to guess where they were, yet the smiling countenances of the shepherds seemed to invite them to inquire into many particulars concerning the way, and were much surprised at the readiness and clearness of their answers.

CLERICUS. We have been informed that there is a city of Refuge, and being assured also that our city was to be destroyed by fire, therefore, journey we in search of the city where we may be safe and happy. Is this the way?

SHEPHERDS. Well, brethren, we are happy to inform you that this is the right way, and these beautiful mountains were prepared by the Lord of the Celestial City, for the refreshment of *pilgrims* previous to their entering the city. And as you seem to be weary, and the day is far spent, turn you in and rest awhile, then go on your journey.

So they consented to tarry with them as they desired, also to look at some of the scenery of the mountains. So they were unostentatiously provided with simple but happy lodgings and fare, and were soon in the embrace of sleep.

CHAPTER XV.

CONVERSATION WITH THE SHEPHERDS—SCENERY OF THE MOUNTAINS—JOURNEY ONWARD.

And He gave some apostles, and prophets, and evangelists, and pastors, and teachers, for the perfecting of the saints.—EPH. iv. 11.

AFTER a most delicious night's repose, interspersed with pleasing dreams, through which the memories of the past, like rippling streams, flowed in pleasing or painful cadence, corresponding to the events revived, the central images of which seemed to be the shepherds and the mountain scenery, mingled with thoughts of the Clelestial City, they awoke, and soon divined the secret of their sweet dreams, as the mountain breezes floated gently in at their upraised window, loaded with the aromatic fragrance of the orchards and vineyards, accompanied by the gentle voices of the shepherds, whom, they discovered, were already abroad, leading their flocks by the still waters of the beautiful river, in the luxuriant pastures there.

So, speedily arranging their wardrobes, they went forth to greet them and enjoy the sweet air.

SHEPHERDS. Hail! brethren; and how enjoyed you your rest?

CLERICUS. Amazingly, good sirs. Never was rest more refreshing, as I think my brethren can testify.

SHEPHERDS. The King is very kind and watchful; and knowing full well the dangers of the way, and the toils of faithful pilgrims, "He giveth his beloved sleep," lest they despair.

PROBUS. Kind sirs, while our hearts overflow with gratitude, we would know of the reports we heard, and also of the way yet before us, for we long to be advancing.

SHEPHERDS. You were rightly informed, and you have done well to hasten to that beautiful city, for we judge, from your appearance, that you have been pressing your journey, and are happy to inform you that you are in the right way. But how got you into this way, and how succeeded you in escaping the many dangers and getting on thus far?

PILGRIM. As I was serving in the city of Destruction, I began to be oppressed with the abounding wickedness, and just then a book fell into my hands, written by men called *ouranographers;* and, as I read, my alarm increased. So I fled from the doomed city, and was directed by one *Evangelist* to enter a little gate at the beginning of the way; and, by the aid of the *Interpreter*, and this good *Evangelist*, we have made our way thus far, although we came near being destroyed by a storm among the mountains, and by the giant Infidel; and, on several other occasions, falling in by the way with men who seemed to be going, as they said, to the city, we were led by them through some very barren country, and along some very steep, dangerous places; but, by the grace of the good Prince, and the instructions we received from the good book which I had found, we are thankful in escaping thus far.

SHEPHERDS. But, Brother *Clericus*, it is not often we see those of your rank on these mountains, where the flocks feed and flourish upon the simple herbs the Lord of the Delectable Mountains has caused to grow here.

CLERICUS. I feel my unworthy self reproved, and yet joyful, in being permitted to be here. No better proof of the healthiness of these herbs, and this atmosphere, is needed than what I see in the condition and harmony of these flocks. Here I see you have the wolf and the lamb, and the leopard and the kid, lying down together (Isa. xi. 6), and the calf and the young lion and the fatling together, and a little child leading them. The cow and the bear eating together, and the lion feeding like the ox, and the suckling creeping to the hole of the asp, and the weaned child putting its hand on the cockatrice's den, and all seems peace and harmony. And I remember with pain, when I dwelt in the city of Orthodoxy, how the streets crossed each other, and how much contention and strife there was, and emulation to see who could get the most numbers and build the finest houses.

SHEPHERDS. But how came you to leave?

CLERICUS. I confess that I became disgusted with such things, and alarmed at the amount of worldly-mindedness I discovered, when laboring to bring about a reconciliation. And some hints, given by *Restorer*, and some other things connected with the visit of Brother *Pilgrim* to our city, induced me to examine the good book more closely, and I soon saw my best plan was to leave all and go where it directed. And I bless Immanuel that my feet are to-day permitted to tread this delightful mountain.

So, after some further conversation, interspersed with many questions to each of them, the shepherds were highly pleased at the indications given that they had sincerely left all and followed in the path that led them to these mountains. They moreover cordially extended their hands to them, and invited them to remain a while, and refresh themselves with the good things of the mountains, when the company joyfully accepted the invitation, as they felt the need of being strengthened for the journey yet before them.

So, after still further delightful conversation, the shepherds took them to walk upon the mountains, that they might show them some of the scenery thereof. So, as they walked forth, they were delighted with the beautiful prospect on every hand. And although the arrangements of the ground were seemingly for beauty alone, so pleasant was it, yet its adaptation to some useful end was also remarkable. Then did the shepherds call their attention to some of the most wonderful points, which made a deep impression upon their minds.

They had them to the top of one very high hill, called Spiritual Pride, and bade them look down— which, when they did, they saw a great number at the bottom dashed all to pieces. And when they inquired what this meant, the shepherds told them these were those who had, from various causes, considered themselves the peculiar favorites of Heaven, and, withal, being a little flattered by the people, had become haughty (1 Tim. iii. 6), and not noticing where they stopped, had walked off this precipice and fallen, while their bodies lie there unburied as a warning to others.

Then they passed on to another high point, whence they saw two groups of men, the one of which seemed to be wandering among the tombs, upon which they frequently stumbled, as those who were blind. These, said the shepherds, like Hymeneus and Philetus (2 Tim. ii. 17), erred concerning the resurrection, claiming that there was no spirit separate from the body, and that the wicked, etc., would be annihilated. The other group seemed also to be gliding about like ones insane. These, said the shepherds, sought unto spirits that peep and mutter. (Isa. viii. 19.) Therefore have they become insane. Take warning from these, and beware of speculating in spiritual things. These poor creatures entered the field of free-thinking, whereinto led a gate, that had been much beautified by human devices on each of its panels, and inscribed with various mottoes, that did much to arrest their attention, and lead them to think that they could reach the Celestial City without the trials of the straight and narrow way that led over these mountains. Therefore they wandered on till they became bewildered and lost, and act as you now see.

Then did the pilgrims feel sad when they thought of their narrow escape, as some of their number had even entered the same field, and were only marvellously delivered. Therefore did they inwardly greatly rejoice, and determine with themselves that they would make the "name of God a lamp to their feet and a light to their path," and follow it only.

The shepherds then led them to another place, where they came abruptly to another curious gate, that at first sight seemed an inviting place to enter, which, when the shepherds had thrown open, they bade them look in, when they saw a path leading along to the left, that at first was pleasant, but then it grew rougher, and at last abruptly terminated in a terrible pit (Matt. xxiv. 51), from which issued groans, and smoke, and the scent of brimstone, whereat the whole company were greatly alarmed. This, the shepherds informed them, was the way that hypocrites always took. They would start on a pilgrimage, enter the right gate, and travel along the right path, make many pretensions to keep up an outside show, but invariably enter this gate and plunge into that pit.

This was, indeed, a fearful picture. Then said—

RESOLUTE. And do you keep these facts from the knowledge of those who journey this way, seeing some might from curiosity enter here, and thus meet this terrible fate?

SHEPHERDS. By no means. On the contrary, we take particular pains to inform all concerning it, and to warn them; nevertheless, many enter whom we do not suspect.

PROBUS. Then how difficult to escape all these dangers, and reach the city!

SHEPHERDS. None enter here unless they choose to, since the *will* is concerned in this matter. "Behold," saith God (Deut. xxx. 15), "I set before thee this day life and good, and death and evil." And every one makes his choice.

Clericus by no means felt happy under the memories awakened by these hints, when he saw in the light of what the kind shepherds said the fearful risk he had been running, when trying to patch up the walls and straighten and harmonize the streets in the city of Orthodoxy, and could not refrain from saying, "Blessed be *Immanuel* that he has opened up a clear way, which, although it lies *through* danger, yet leads *from* greater dangers, and grows brighter and brighter. And blessed be his name for placing kind shepherds along this way, to encourage weary travellers. I see other interesting views around these delightful mountains—one, in particular, that seems to be enticing—and yet I would be on our journey.

PILGRIM. Yes, dear brethren, I seem to feel a

strangely anxious emotion mingling with the increasing pleasures afforded by the shepherds' entertainments (Phil. ii. 12), and I am much of Brother *Clericus's* mind.

SHEPHERDS. Nor would we detain you, but as we have now arrived near the inviting spot noticed by Brother *Clericus,* we would that you should take one view from thence ere you depart. So leading them up quite a lofty eminence, from which new and thrilling beauties presented themselves as they rose; they at length came to a beautiful observatory, where was a telescope of very peculiar powers, which brought into a clearer light things unseen by the naked eye. (2 Cor. iv. 18.) The shepherds desired them to look through the glass, which, when they had done, they saw a highway cast up and beautifully paved, winding among the distant hills, and along verdant vales, and through beautiful landscapes, until it seemed to come to a large white gate made of pearl (Rev. xxi. 21), that glistened with its resplendent purity. They thought they saw also above the gate shining ones, and beyond a lofty wall of variegated brilliants (Rev. xxi. 19) that stretched either way from the gate—lofty palaces and thrones that seemed to float in a strange and wonderous light that came neither from the sun, or moon, or stars, nor any candle. (Rev. xxi. 23.) They also thought they heard entrancing strains of music (Rev. xiv. 2), as joyful voices mingled with tones of harps. And as they gazed, they seemed to be enraptured, and *Probus* burst forth in singing, joined by the rest—

> "My soul would always stay,
> In such a frame as this,
> And sit and sing itself away
> To everlasting bliss."

And when they would now go forward, being anxious to arrive at that beautiful city, the *shepherds* took them by the hand and bade them beware of Theologos (Col. ii. 8), and not to sleep upon the Enchanted grounds. (1 Cor. x. 7.) And to give good heed to the directions of the "Reports" Pilgrim had brought with him. (2 Pet. i. 19.)

So with many expressions of gratitude and sympathy, they took each other by the hand and parted. The whole company seemed unusually happy, and moved with much greater ease after this interview, and felt that somehow the very memory of their former trials and dangers added pleasure to their present bliss, as they were mingled with thoughts of that wonderous city they had just seen ahead, and the many assurances of the progress they had made, and encouragement that they should soon be at their journey's end.

CHAPTER XVI.

INTERVIEWS BY THE WAY—ENCHANTED GROUND.

We have also a more sure word of prophecy, whereunto ye do well that ye take heed as unto a light that shineth in a dark place, until the day dawn and the day-star arise in your hearts.—2 PET. i. 19.

THE country through which they now passed was beautiful and well cultivated, and all conspired to make their journey delightful. The weather being pleasant they made good progress, while their minds were filled with happy thoughts about the arrangements and order and beauty of the Delectable Mountains.

CLERICUS. Brethren, it appears to me that the order pursued by the *shepherds*, is much more simple and effective than any thing I ever saw in the city of *Orthodoxy*.

PILGRIM. And so natural and beautiful! It reminded me of all I heard *Mr. Restorer* say, and of that beautiful hymn—

"Thus shall the church below,
Resemble that above."

Certainly nothing is more desirable than that we should be subject to the same order on earth, that we shall be in heaven. It would not be safe to *square* us by one rule and *judge* us by another.

PROBUS. Yes, its simplicity was its chief attraction. They seemed to have no will or ambitious desires of their own. All was humble submission to the Divine Will.

RESOLUTE. The very atmosphere seemed purer, and the gates of the Celestial City could almost be seen with the naked eye—it seemed as if I could always remain with them. How true

"The hill of Zion yields,
A thousand sacred sweets,
Before we reach the heavenly fields,
Or walk the golden streets."

But it seems to me the country before us descends rapidly and does not seem so pleasant.

PROBUS. See! off there to the right what a beautiful little village. The main buildings seem large for such a sized village. And what a delightful path leads from it, embowered with venerable elms and flowering shrubs;—and see, there comes a prim-looking gentleman in black, walking daintily along the path that seems to cross the road ahead of us.

CLERICUS. That scene looks familiar to me; it was at that place I received my education, and that gentleman resembles the son of a fellow-townsman in the city of Orthodoxy, who has been here a long time, and if report says right, has arisen to some eminence, filling one of the most important chairs in the Institution.

PILGRIM. He seems to be coming into our path ahead of us, so let us quicken our pace that we may make some inquiries of him,—it may be we may learn something to our advantage.

So hurrying along they soon drew near, as their paths seemed to run together for some distance, when Resolute thus addressed the stranger.

Sir, you seem to come from yonder beautiful village, and it may be you are well acquainted with the country, and could give some useful information to a band of pilgrims, in reference to their journey to the *Celestial City*.

STRANGER. All hail! brethren, you have judged rightly, although not a native here yet I have spent many years within yonder classic walls, and have also itinerated much of the country around, and am not only quite well acquainted with that, but have made the route to the *Celestial City* my especial study, and shall be glad to communicate any information in reference to it you may desire.

CLERICUS. Were you not from the city of *Orthodoxy*.

STRANGER. I was, and my father resides there still.

CLERICUS. Is not your name *Theologos*, son of old Father *Divinity*, Rector of a Parish there.

STRANGER. The same, at your service, sir. But may I inquire if you were acquainted in the city of Orthodoxy, and with my father?

CLERICUS. Well acquainted with both, sir. I was born there and your father was my tutor.

THEOLOGOS. Did you not belong to the family of *Mr. Clergy?* and what brings you here?

CLERICUS. I did, and you may have heard something of my efforts to harmonize the different *streets*, and bring about a more friendly feeling.

THEOLOGOS. Yes, sir. My father wrote to me that you had called a *world's convention*, to see if some *creed* could not be compiled from all the *creeds* upon which all might unite, and at one time my father expressed a faint hope that you might succeed. But when he saw how tenaciously each one clung to their own, he gave the matter a closer consideration, and concluded that it would be better to maintain their separate organizations, and says, when he presented his conclusions, the rest generally agreed with him.

CLERICUS. I soon saw that the effort was abortive, and so gave it up, and concluded I would leave the city of Orthodoxy and journey to the *Celestial City*.

THEOLOGOS. You do not mean to say it was necessary to leave *orthodoxy* and *creeds*, in order to get to the Celestial City. Do you?

CLERICUS. I will say, sir, the moment I came to the above conclusion, I had new and strange feelings and saw with new eyes. I had thought that *creeds* and *parties* were at least *innocent*. But then I saw and read clearly in the *Bible*, that they were *carnal* (1 Cor. iii. 4) and wicked, and that the Great Head of the church had ordained that all his followers should walk by the same rule (Phil. iii. 16), and that there should be no divisions among them. (1 Cor. i. 10.)

THEOLOGOS. But, my dear brethren, you do not mean to say that these different *organizations* and *de-*

nominations constitute the divisions forbidden, and that different *creeds* are different *rules?*

CLERICUS. Well, if they are not, I would not know what it would take to constitute such.

THEOLOGOS. But are they not all agreed in the great fundamental items of Evangelical religion—the necessity of the new birth and entire sanctification, with the equal Divinity of the Three adorable persons in the Godhead?

CLERICUS. No, sir. I found when an effort was made to harmonize them, that it called forth such fine spun distinctions and Ashdodish terms, that proved they differed vitally and could not be reconciled.

THEOLOGOS. Oh! it is true, each *branch* of the church has its different *views* of the saving *doctrines* of the Bible, and these *creeds* only serve to show the world the peculiar views of each *branch,* but do not interfere with the authority of the Scriptures.

CLERICUS. True, they do not interfere with the *authority* of the word of God, which I rejoice to know is as firm as his throne. But then these *peculiar views* are made their *tests* of fellowship and *standards* of orthodoxy, and are as clearly the "rules of faith and practice," to these *branches,* as the writings of the apostles were to the primitive church; moreover, they seem to multiply and perpetuate those very divisions forbidden in the Scripture, thus crippling the Gospel, neutralizing the efforts of the church, filling the world with infidels, and bringing religion into disgrace.

THEOLOGOS. But, sir, every denomination must have its *creed*, written or unwritten, or how shall the world know where to find them. It does not matter so much what they believe, if the heart is only right. When we get to the Celestial City it will not be asked of us what *fold* we lived in. But I was going out to meet an appointment in a neighboring Parish, and I see we are approaching the point where my path crosses and turns to the left of your road, and I should be glad to have you accompany me.

PROBUS. Friend *Theologos*, does your Parish lay on the direct road to the *Celestial City?*

THEOLOGOS. Well, not on what you call the direct road, but a road leads from there to the city, and I don't think when we get there it will be asked of us what road we came.

PROBUS. True, but you seem to have too many ifs; and after all our troubles and dangers, we want to make sure work. If there are various roads we want the right one, and most direct. We feel that our time is too short and precious to make experiments.

PILGRIM. (Taking out the volume of reports). Do you think this "Travellers' Guide" will give us correct directions, and enable us to find the way to the *City*.

THEOLOGOS. Oh! yes. That I see is the New Testament. It is the only true foundation of faith and practice, but then—

RESOLUTE. But then, Friend Theologos, you think it needs construing.

THEOLOGOS. I think—I mean—let every one take his own way and sail under his own flag.

RESOLUTE. So say I, but I am determined to sail under the blood-stained banner of the *Good Prince*, and walk in the way marked out by the Prophets and Apostles.

THEOLOGOS. Farewell, brethren. I must take down this lane.

So saying, he turned to the left, and the company passed on some distance in silence. At length *Probus*, started from a deep reverie, on the interview they had just had, and said, I think, brethren, this must be the man the shepherds warned us of. But it seems to me, after feasting on such food as the shepherds provide, there is but little danger of being satisfied with such unsavory stuff as this man's.

CLERICUS. True, Brother Probus; but all do not see to the bottom of things as you do, and thousands are deceived by such specious logic; and hence sectarianism flourishes at the expense of true religion.

PILGRIM. This reminds me of what I read in the reports (2 Thess. ii. 9, 10) concerning the *man of sin*—"Even him whose coming is after the working of Satan, with all deceivableness, of unrighteousness, in them that perish, because they receive not the lore of the truth, that they might be saved." And this same power is said to have attempted so to fix it that none should buy or sell save those who have the mark of the beast (Rev. xiii. 17); that is, I suppose, as Theologos intimated, that none should be recognized as orthodox, or allowed into orthodox pulpits, save those who had a creed.

CLERICUS. Well, such seems to have been the working of creeds, in a measure. None are allowed to buy or sell, or enjoy religious intercourse with the self-styled orthodox but those whom they consider evangelical—that is, have a creed.

RESOLUTE. But it appears to me, brethren, that the air is oppressive, and I greatly incline to sleep.

PILGRIM. I should judge, from appearances, that night is coming on; and see! from these milestones, we have journeyed a long distance, and I was suffering from the same feelings.

As it grew darker, clouds and fog arose, insomuch that they were much troubled to find the road, and they earnestly sought a place of rest. Yet *Clericus* exhorted them to continue on, as he had strong suspicions they were on the *Enchanted ground.*

CHAPTER XVII.

STILL ON THE ENCHANTED GROUND—RECEIVE LETTERS FROM EVANGELIST—ARE SCATTERED.

Wherefore, let him that thinketh he standeth take heed lest he fall. There hath no temptation taken you but such as is common to man; but God is faithful, who will not suffer you to be tempted above that you are able, but will, with the temptation, also make a way to escape. 1 COR. x. 12, 13.

THE night seemed to wear wearily on, yet they found no place of rest, while the warning of the shepherds came up in their minds to stimulate them forward, and a thousand ominous apprehensions filled their minds, and boding fears, of various sorts, made their hearts throb and their whole frame to tremble. So they endeavored to cheer each other what they could, to keep awake.

All at once a voice broke through the horrid gloom, saying, "There hath no temptation taken you but such as is common to man; but God is faithful, who will not suffer you to be tried above that ye are able, but will, with the temptation, also make a way to escape." Then said—

Clericus. My brethren, who can doubt the source of this *voice?* Let us, therefore, not be discouraged, but patiently wait for the coming of the day.

Again the same voice said, "My grace shall be sufficient for thee." But still the darkness grew apace, and seemed to be all the more dreary from their remembrance of the *Delectable Mountains* and its beautiful scenery.

And, withal, they began to grow cold and drowsy, and peevish with each other. Nor did they seem inclined to converse together as freely as heretofore, or even to take delight in each other's company. So they separated, and walked at some distance from each other, when that *voice* was again heard, saying, "There must be also heresies among you, that they which are approved may be made manifest." (1 Cor. xi. 19.) This seemed to fill them with much anxiety, and, as they wandered on thus in the dark, each was left to commune with his own heart.

Clericus threw himself upon his knees, deeply bewailing his unworthiness, begging for pardon and wisdom and guidance. *Pilgrim* was almost in despair. He turned this way, and then that, feeling after the path with his staff, uncertain where to tread. *Resolute* went on like a lion, in the dark, although he felt deeply the loss of company, and had some conflict of soul; yet he could not feel that he was to blame, when a *hobgoblin*, tripping up behind him, whispered in his ear, "If you yield one inch, the world will think you are to blame. This darkness and trouble is all brought on by others." So he thought it was the voice of his own conscience, and determined to brave it through.

Poor *Probus*, finding that he was not making much progress, sat down on a mossy knoll to meditate. He went back to the beginning of their journey; he thought of the fate of those pleasure-seeking freethinkers, and those in *Infidel Castle*, of the sad fate of those who had turned aside, of the gloomy prospects of the inhabitants of the city of *Destruction*, and then he came in his thoughts to the beautiful river and orchards and scenes they had passed, the joys at *Berea*, and on the *Delectable Mountains*, and, finally, the glimpse they had of the gates of the *Celestial City*, and felt that they could not be far ahead, and as he pondered the tears ran down; yet courage reigned in his heart, for he knew this gloom could not last always. Just then, as if a clap of thunder had burst over the valley, the same familiar *voice* was heard: "These light afflictions, which are but for a moment, shall work out a far more exceeding and eternal weight of glory, for all things shall work together for your good."

Indeed, as when the dark storm-cloud, broken in mid-heavens by the violence of the wind that brought it there, discharges its contents and is then driven away, so the darkness began to disappear; and, indeed, it soon grew so light that the pilgrims descried each other, at no great distance apart, and, as if by a common impulse, ran together, and falling upon each other's necks, mutually bewailed this strange event, and falling upon their knees, implored divine aid, and promised to aid each other to the end of their journey.

The day broke, the sun came forth and shone with more splendor than ever, while the landscape, as they ascended from the valley, was more beautiful than ever.

So they went on joyfully, and soon came to the next town, a beautiful city, where they found a large number of brethren assembled from all parts of the land in a general *missionary meeting*. This was indeed a very happy season, to see so many gray-haired pilgrims just ripe for the *Celestial City*, and a still larger number of earnest young brethren, girding their loins for the harvest of the world. They found, also, that the *telegraph* and *mail* had preceded them, and their history was in a great measure known. Indeed, the *corresponding secretary* had received a letter from *Evangelist*, signed by order of a number of churches, recommending them to the work of the

Lord, as veterans who had endured toils and hardships, and had proved themselves worthy and willing to be spent in the same service.

This filled them with amazement; but when the *society*, by a unanimous voice, called them to the work, they submitted, promising to give their feeble all to it.

Then, with many prayers and tears, the brethren, amid great rejoicings, gave them the "right hand of fellowship," and sent them forth.

The time had now come when they must separate, perhaps not to meet again till they should arrive at the *Celestial City;* still they parted cheerfully and affectionately, feeling assured that—

> "The same hand that led them
> Through scenes dark and drear,
> Would kindly conduct them safe home."

It also appeared, from other letters received during the meeting, that, stimulated by their example, scores had left the cities of *Destruction* and *Orthodoxy*, and even the enchanting field of *free-thinking*, and *doubting*, and *infidel castles*, and other places, and started on pilgrimage, many of whom had got the start of them, and reached the *Celestial City*, and that many others were seriously thinking of setting out; and thus, when they least expected, their chaste conversation, coupled with fear, together with their persevering and consistent course, had led others to glorify God by a consecration to his service.

CHAPTER XVIII.

CLOSING INCIDENTS—BLESSEDNESS OF DIVINE PROMISES—THE ROD AND STAFF OF GOD—OVER THE RIVER.

But none of these things move me, neither count I my life dear unto myself, so that I might finish my course with joy.—ACTS xx. 24.

BUT it soon became apparent, notwithstanding the joy of their hearts, and the cheering reports of the triumphs of truth on every hand, that the *black prince* was yet abroad; neither had he manifested a disposition to yield the struggle or cease his wiles to annoy and take the lives of these good men. And on their part, although they were growing gray in the service, they had no intention of giving up, for that, indeed, a knowledge of the exposed and dangerous condition of their friends and neighbors filled them with a desire to do all in their power to aid and save them. And now that they were commissioned and encouraged to go abroad everywhere, preaching the word, they separated and went forward with the more eagerness.

As for *Resolute,* he had not gone far before he received a letter, requesting him to come and hold a meeting in a village called *Careless,* in the State of *Indifference.* The circumstances were like this: *Mr. Evangelist* had passed through that country, and produced a great sensation by his preaching, and a large church had been formed; but, being left to themselves, they became a prey to various teachers, which had so distracted the minds of the people that they had become discouraged, and religion had pretty much run out. But a young man by the name of *Honest*, who remained faithful to the profession he had made under the preaching of *Evangelist*, became greatly concerned for the salvation of his neighbors, and so had written to the meeting to have some *missionary* sent down there, to see if they could not be aroused, which letter was forwarded to *Resolute*. So he proceeded at once to the place, and being a stranger, he called at the *Weathercock Inn*, kept by one *Fair-speech*, who gave a very glowing description of the place, its fine air, fertile soil, beautiful situation, excellent opportunities, together with the good health and general prosperity of the inhabitants. This seemed strange to *Resolute*, as it was known to be barren and destitute of water, with a bad air, filled with a miasm that caused giddiness in the head and general lassitude of spirits; and as to its opportunities, he had seen nothing but dreary marshes, gloomy forests, and a sandy desert. So, concealing his surprise at the strange hallucination of the landlord, he inquired the name of the country off to the right as he came into the village. *Fair-speech* told him that was called *Calvinian Moor*, in honor of a gentleman who first settled there, who, finding it very miry, had undertaken to fill it up and render the ground firmer; but although they had got it in such state of cultivation that they raised a few things for market, yet men and animals were occasionally mired there. The extensive forest on your right is called *Arminian Woods,* in honor to another man who had dwelt there. Their posterity built this city, and then many of them went on and settled the vast region of country that lies beyond on the other side of the city, which you will pass through when you go on. That is called *Universalian Desert.*

But, said *Resolute,* have you any churches in your little city?

Well, as to that, said *Fair-speech,* a *Mr. Evangelist* held a meeting here some years ago, and caused quite a stir, inducing a great many to join him, but the inhabitants of the surrounding country rallying, the thing was measurably checked; and their views and theories, when mixed together, resulted in such a multiplicity of doctrines, that I think the people generally concluded they would be better off without troubling themselves about religion at all. Since then we have had comparative quiet and prosperity.

RESOLUTE. Your quiet is the quiet of death, and your prosperity that which will lead you to endless ruin. But is there one *Honest* in your city?

FAIR-SPEECH. Yes, and an excellent, thoughtful, exemplary young man he is. He lives down on *Christian street,* a name given in honor of the church *Evangelist* organized there.

So saying, he led *Resolute* to the corner, and, by request, pointed out the house to him.

Here *Resolute* was heartily welcomed, and, with many prayers and tears, they took sweet counsel together. And as they talked of the languishing state of Zion, and the sad ruin wrought by the conflicting theories and impracticable doctrines of men, they resolved to make another effort to erect the Gospel standard, and call men simply to the obedience of faith (Rom. xvi. 26), believing that although difficulties might be in the way, yet it was better to fall struggling, with all their armor on and gain a crown, than ignominiously to fly and fall wounded in the back and sink in disgrace for ever.

And sure enough, with such a mind as this they could but prosper. Many were revived; scores flocked to the standard of *Prince Immanuel.* Those who came from *Calvinian Moor*, and *Arminian Woods*, and the *desert*, alike testified to the superior joys they felt on taking the word of God as the only rule of faith and practice, to those dreamy impressions and vague philosophies upon which they had before tried to rest. They felt that all things necessary to life and godliness was given to them through the knowledge of Christ (2 Pet. i. 3) which they found in the Bible, and that all the creeds and opinions of men only tended to unsettle the mind and cause divisions, while with one heart and one voice they glorified God for the blessed promise, "He that believeth, and is baptized, shall be saved." (Mark xvi. 16.) "Yes," said *Resolute*, "say not in thine heart, Who shall ascend into heaven?—that is, to bring down Christ from above; or, Who shall descend into the deep?—that is, to bring Christ up again from the dead; but, The word is nigh thee, even in thy mouth and in thy heart; that is, the word of faith which we preach.

That if thou shalt confess with thy mouth the Lord Jesus, and shalt believe in thine heart that God hath raised him from the dead, thou shalt be saved." (Rom. x. 6.) "And with many other words did he testify and exhort, saying, Save yourselves from this untoward generation." (Acts. ii. 40.)

So when he had set things in order, and solemnly charged them to keep the ordinances as they were delivered unto them (1 Cor. xi. 2), and to do all things without murmurings and disputings (Phil. ii. 14), that they might be the sons of God, without rebuke, shining as lights in the world, he departed. Young *Honest* accompanied him some distance on his journey, as he must needs pass along near the *desert.*

Now, it came to pass, as they journeyed on, having their conversation in heaven (Ph. iii. 20), that *Resolute* being in a happy frame of mind, soon caught sight of the *river,* from which he had drank so often and been refreshed. And as he was sweetly discoursing of the satisfying nature of those waters (1 Jo. v. 4), the wind began to rise and the clouds to gather over the *desert,* when the sand began to move; for it was so, that there was no vegetation (Jo. xv. 4.), since the inhabitants thought it not very necessary to be particular in keeping the commandments, as they thought it would be well with all in the end, any way. But now it seemed that this little *monsoon* would stifle the inhabitants. Some were even seen running in the direction of the road, where the two friends were walking, and as they drew near they cried out, what shall we do! Whereupon, *Resolute* told them they must throw themselves into the river, calling upon the name of the Lord. (Acts xxii. 16.) And noticing there was some of the *leaves* and *mud* from the *forest* and *heath* on them, he told them the waters of the river would also wash these all off. Being now driven to an extremity, they were most willing to do this, inasmuch as they were also very thirsty. And as the sand continued to threaten, and others flocked around, *Resolute* took them by the hand and went down with them into the river (Acts viii. 38), when, to their inexpressible surprise and joy, the wind abated and the sand settled. The storm being now past, they told *Resolute* that some of them had been born in *Arminian Wood*, and some on *Calvinian Heath*, and others even in the city of Orthodoxy, but from a restless spirit of adventure they had removed and settled on this *sand*, as they had been told it was an easy matter to make a living there. But they found the sunshine and drought so constant there, that it pulverized the dust, and when a little storm arose, it was sent blinding through the air, and they were now desirous of seeking a better location, when *Resolute* advised them to settle along the river, and encouraged *Honest* to assist them in forming a settlement.

Resolute, bidding them an affectionate farewell, passed on, and soon found himself on the *Plain of Obedience*, through which the beautiful river wended, as he kept the road that led along its bank.

The air was fresh and delightful, the birds sung sweetly in the orchards, which again began to appear, interspersed with vineyards, now loading the air with the smell of ripened fruit. And, withal, *Resolute* caught a glimpse through the trees that skirted the sloping hillside in the distance before him, of the *Celestial City*. This so filled his soul with rapture, that in the joyful anticipation thereof he fell sick and turned into a pleasant dwelling by the way-side, inhabited by a noble family, long a resident of this delightful *plain*.

These received him joyfully and showed him every kindness, anticipating all his wants. But such was his calm and holy resignation and the loving style of his conversation, which turned altogether upon the *city*, and its glories, and honors, and joys, that they felt as though they were greatly his debtors whenever he expressed any gratitude for little acts of kindness.

Indeed, the affliction of *Resolute* waxed so rapidly that the family grew alarmed, when he exhorted them to be of good cheer, for he said, "none of these things disturb me, neither count I my life dear unto me (Phil. iii. 8), so that I may come to the gates of the beautiful city I see just before me; not in the righteousness of the law, but clothed with that righteousness which is required in the Gospel. Long have I lived and labored; but forgetting the things that are behind, I press towards the *Celestial City*, whose pearly gates I see shining before me."

A solemn impression prevailed, as this veteran of the cross dwelt upon these exceeding great and precious promises, which now acted as a staff of God (Psa. xxiii. 4), given to sustain under His rod, when it seemed as if sweet strains of music floated through the air, "Great and marvellous are thy works, Lord God Almighty, just and true are thy ways, thou King of saints. (Rev. xv. 3.) Who shall not fear thee, O Lord, and glorify thy name, for thou art holy, for all nations shall come and worship before thee, for thy judgments are made manifest."

Upon this, *Resolute* roused him a little, and said gently—

"Hark they whisper! angels say,
Sister spirit come away."

Then he desired them, as they stood calmly around his bed, to sing this hymn—

"Sing me to my last sweet slumber,
For my eyes are growing dim;
Let me hear before I close them,
Some familiar solemn hymn.
Let it be no strain of sadness,
Telling of distrust and fear;
Doubt has in my heart no dwelling,
For I feel my Saviour near.

"Sing me to my last sweet slumber
Hope is bright, and faith is strong;
And my spirit feels like soaring
Upward on the wings of song.
Death for me has now no terror,
And the grave hath lost its gloom,
Since o'er death the Saviour triumphed
On the morn he left the tomb

"Sing me to my last sweet slumber,
That the last of earth may be,
But a prelude to the welcome
Of angelic minstrelsy.

Let it be a song of triumph,
  For I soon shall join the strain,
Which is ever sung in heaven
  By the bright redeemed train."

[Wm. Baxter.

And as they ceased, Resolute bade each an affectionate farewell, exhorting them to be faithful until death. Then folding his hands over his breast, gently passed over the river.

Tears flowed freely, but in silence, from all that stood around, and many a wish swelled every heart, "Let me die the death of the righteous, and let my last end be like his." (Num. xxiii. 10.) His beloved remains were followed to the silent grave by a large and deeply solemn concourse.

CHAPTER XIX.

FALSE PREMISES LEAD TO FALSE CONCLUSIONS — SOVEREIGNTY—FAITH—FREE-WILL — SANCTIFICATION— PROBUS CROSSES THE RIVER.

But they, measuring themselves by themselves, and comparing themselves among themselves, are not wise.—2 Cor. x. 12.

Poor *humanity* is strangely bewildered, having lost its common centre of attraction in *Christ*. Each one seeks a centre in himself, or, wildly zigzagging, crosses everybody else's track; and thus an endless confusion will reign, until again restored to their rightful allegiance to the *Lord* and centre of the spiritual universe, whose divine sovereignty alone can restore order.

Now *Probus,* although of an inquisitive and speculative turn of mind, yet from the time he was brought to see the truth, as it was in Jesus, would not suffer himself to be led by *carnal reason,* or *opinions,* alleging that these were what had caused and still kept up the divisions in the religious world, and maintained that the word of God alone, properly interpreted, was the *only rule of faith and practice,* so that, as a missionary, he had a very important work to perform, and one much needed; nor was he slow in performing his task. Nor was he merely successful in turning many souls from darkness to light, but such was his zeal in overthrowing everything that exalted itself against the truth, that he obtained the sobriquet of *Iconoclast,* or destroyer of creeds.

One day, as he was passing near a city called *Neapolis,* he overtook three clerical-looking gentlemen, by the names of *Dr. Decree,* and *Mr. Experience,* and *Demure,* who saluted him civilly, and invited him to join their company.

PROBUS. Gentlemen, you seem to have come from yonder city. Might I be permitted to inquire its name?

DR. DECREE. That, sir, is called *Neapolis,* a *new city,* built on the road from the city of *Orthodoxy* to the *City of God,* and on a more liberal plan than the former. The inhabitants of the different streets are on very friendly terms, and the ministers even exchange pulpits, especially on great occasions, as we have agreed to disagree; or, rather, not to let our little differences hinder such a neighborly intercourse.

DEMURE. Might I be permitted to ask to what branch of the Christian church you belong?

PROBUS. I belong to the church itself, and not to a branch. I understand each disciple of Christ is a branch of Christ or his church. (Jo. xv. 5.)

EXPERIENCE. Very true, sir; but then it is necessary to have names for the different churches, in order to distinguish them; and you have no right to claim the name *Christian*, because that would unchristianize us, and I trust we are all good Christians, although we go by different names.

PROBUS. As to that, I am not to judge; but if my being only what I ought to be unchristianizes you, see ye to that. Christ has espoused the church unto himself as his bride (2 Cor. xi. 2), and woe to him who would separate between husband and wife, or the wife who would dishonor her husband by going by another name.

DR. DECREE. Well, brethren, there is nothing in a name. "A rose, by any other name would smell as sweet." But the great matter is to have the heart right and the faith *orthodox*.

PROBUS. Sir, I know not that I understand you. The heart, if I understand it, is regulated by the faith, and faith should be based on the word of God.

DEMURE. I presume the *Doctor* means that those cardinal articles received by all evangelical churches are orthodox, and that the heart is right when it is filled with holy desires by the Holy Ghost, which thrusts out all money-changers.

Dr. Decree. Yes, sir, man was made upright; but, by the fall, he was corrupted, body, soul, and spirit, and made subject to death, temporal, spiritual, and eternal, with no power of his own to repent, think one good thought, speak one good word, or perform one good deed, totally depraved.

Probus. Then of what virtue are the commands of God, calling upon him to believe and repent?

Dr. Decree. True, the ways of God are mysterious; but in the divine sovereignty, through the influence of the Holy Spirit, he brings all to the saving benefits of the atonement, who were chosen in Christ before the foundation of the world.

Probus. Do you mean to say the divine sovereignty was manifest, first, in choosing a select few, before the foundation of the world, and, second, in bringing them by an irresistible influence to a knowledge of the truth?

Dr. Decree. Yes; God has a right to do as seemeth good to him. "Therefore hath he mercy on whom he will, and whom he will he hardeneth." (Rom. ix. 18.) But the fact that the elect only are included in the covenant of grace does no injustice to the non-elect, since *uncovenanted* love is forfeited by one single act of transgression, it being based upon the *character*, and not the person; hence, is justly forfeited by one single sin of the non-elect, as in the case of the fallen angels; but *covenant love*, being based upon the *person* of the elect, can never be forfeited, but even their sins shall work greater good to them than though they had not sinned; hence St. Paul "thanked God that the elect had sinned" (Rom. vi. 17), and again, that although one sin works death in the non-elect, yet many and repeated offences in the elect only work justification to life. (Rom. v. 17.)

PROBUS. What, then, are we to understand by Christ's dying for all (2 Cor. v. 15), and commanding all men, everywhere, to repent (Acts xvii. 30), with a promise to all who do, that they shall be saved.

DR. DECREE. This, sir, can only include the elect, because this salvation is not of works, lest any man should boast, but sovereign grace is manifest toward the elect, by bestowing upon them the special gift of faith. This is termed being under grace, while the non-elect are said to be under law; hence they will be judged by the law, or strict justice, and of course condemned, for by the law can no flesh be justified; but the elect are not under law, but under grace.

PROBUS. Well, Brother *Demure*, do you accept this as *orthodox* faith?

DEMURE. As the *Doctor* has said, one item in the law of *Neapolis* is, we agree to disagree; and although I regard this feature of the *Doctor's* faith as a most horrible, abominable, God-dishonoring doctrine, yet, after all, it may be merely technical, since he holds to the main, most glorious doctrine, that we are justified by faith alone.

PROBUS. Might I inquire what you mean by being justified by faith alone?

DEMURE. I mean, sir, that as there are various

kinds of faith, such as historical, scriptural, evangelical, saving, objective, subjective, doctrinal, etc., God, in compassion to our utter helplessness, puts justifying faith into the hearts of those who yield to the gracious influences of his Spirit. As Saint Paul saith, "It is the gift of God." (Eph. ii. 5.)

PROBUS. I read that salvation is the gift of God and also the Holy Spirit and eternal life (Rom. ii. 7), but how does he give faith?

EXPERIENCE. If I may be permitted to speak, it is better felt than told. God's gracious Spirit finds us in our sins, strives with our wicked hearts till it breaks down their icy stubbornness, and then infuses faith into our hearts, which enables us to believe to the saving of our souls.

PROBUS. But I cannot see that your doctrine leaves the sinner any more free or responsible than *Dr. Decree's*, since both leave man at the mercy of what you call the divine sovereignty. If this influence be irresistible, and faith a special bestowal, then how can man be responsible? But Paul says, "faith comes by hearing the word of God" (Rom. x. 17), and James says, "draw near to God, and he will draw near to you" (Jas. iv. 8), "cleanse your hands, you sinners, and purify your hearts, ye double-minded." Evidently, it was for God to open the way and provide the means; but is not man responsible for making use of those means, and walking in that way?

DEMURE. Doth not Saint Paul say that "in me—that is, in my flesh—dwelleth no good thing?" Why, sir, you seem to think we can, of ourselves, repent and purify our hearts and work out our own salvation.

PROBUS. I was simply quoting the Scriptures, and inquiring as to the extent of our ability.

DEMURE. Ability! Sir, I agree with the *Doctor*, that we have no ability to do anything toward our salvation; and yet, by the sanctifying influence of the Holy Ghost, the soul is brought to see its own utter vileness and helplessness; and when a full consciousness that all efforts, resolutions, cries, and strugglings for holiness are as vain as the efforts of the Ethiopian to wash white, is given to it, and the soul is led to look to Christ by faith alone, and to feel its dependence on him for holiness of heart and life, then, as in the twinkling of an eye, just as full a sense of the all-sufficiency of Christ to cleanse and impart his own purity and holiness to the sinner is given. Thus a gracious ability is imparted, and the soul sanctified.

PROBUS. Do I understand you to say that this sanctification is *entire* and *instantaneous*, and all the work of the Holy Ghost?

DEMURE. Yes. However long the mind may have been under conviction, yet this *point*, this decision, is instantaneous. I call it *Christian perfection*, because it is not perfection *completed*, but *begun*.

PROBUS. But, *Doctor*, do I understand that you also accept this as orthodox?

DR. DECREE. I accept, I approve—I mean with some slight technical modifications I admit—that it is all the work of the Spirit, performed for the elect, and yet not wholly independent of man's will, because all moral action springs from the will, and is absolutely holy or unholy, as God or the world shall be chosen. When God is chosen, this emotion of the soul is uppermost, and all the actions of the soul are holy. When the world is chosen—that is, uppermost, and all is sinful, so that when the soul is brought to this willing, holy frame by the power of the Spirit of God—it is absolutely holy, and "cannot sin, because it is born of God." (1 Jo. iii. 9.)

EXPERIENCE. True, there are technical differences; but then the blessed experience is the same. All agree that sanctification is by faith alone. There may be diversities of operations, but all the work of the self-same Spirit. And he that does not receive this great cardinal, evangelical truth, is not *orthodox.*

PROBUS. Well, gentlemen, we will not prolong this discussion. I presume you agree with me that "God has concluded all under sin, that he may have mercy upon all" (Rom. xi. 32); moreover, that he treats the sinner as a responsible party in this matter; that he has set life and death before them; that he calls upon them to believe (Acts xvi. 31), to repent, and be baptized (Acts ii. 38), to lay hold on the hope set before them in the Gospel (Heb. vi. 18); and that, having obeyed from the heart that form of doctrine (which doctrine was the death, burial, and resurrection of Christ, prefigured by repentance and immersion) which was delivered, being then made free from sin, they become servants to God, have their fruits unto holiness, and the end everlasting life (Rom. vi.); servants in the sense of responsible moral agents; and that if they will add to their faith courage, knowledge, temperance, patience, godliness, brotherly kindness, and charity (2 Pet. i. 7), they shall have an abundant entrance into the everlasting kingdom of our Lord and Saviour Jesus Christ. As to your *orthodox* agreements or disagreements, you will have to build many *Neapolises* before you can produce harmony, while your premises are all wrong.

You must give up this scholastic jargon and vain confidence in the doctrines and creeds of men, broken cisterns that can hold no water, and drink of the river of pure and perennial truth found only in the *Living Oracles,* which alone can make wise unto salvation, and afford to the wandering mind of man a centre of attraction, an anchor hold for the aching heart, a sure foundation to build our hopes upon.

As Probus thus waxed warm, the three cried out with one voice—a reformer—heretic—infidel—and putting spurs to their horses, were soon out of sight.

Now *Probus,* somewhat wearied, went again to the river (for he took good care to keep near it) and drank, whereat he was much refreshed. And being now strengthened, he made rapid progress over the *Plain of Obedience,* looking ever and anon to the deep dark *river* that rolled its waters along its furthest boundaries, separating the *plain* from the *Celestial City,* and as night drew on he descried a beautiful little village just ahead. Thither he wended his way, and was joyfully surprised to find his old friend *Evangelist,* smiling and active as ever, with other brethren, whom he learned were holding a glorious meeting, and was easily persuaded to tarry with them a few days. The time spent in sweet converse about the *Celestial City* and its joys and employments passed rapidly by. When Probus in the midst of their discourse one day, as they sat at a table spread with the choicest dainties of the *plain*, suddenly exclaimed, "I am in a strait betwixt two, having a desire to depart and cross the *river*, nevertheless I would like to remain also and enjoy your endearing society." (Ph. i. 23.) Such was his earnestness, that they were taken by surprise and greatly troubled. Nevertheless, when his face was as though he would go forward, all eyes were filled with tears, and they proposed to accompany him to the *river*. So on the morrow, as the day was unusually fine, they all went down to the *river* with him, and they saw the other side completely lined with *shining ones* waiting to welcome him over, while they caught the glad strains of ten thousand voices mingled with the sweet music of golden harps, and saw myriads of waving palms.

"Ah!" said *Probus*, while the very look of heaven beamed in his countenance, "We are come unto Mount Zion, and unto the city of the living God, the heavenly Jerusalem, and to an innumerable company of angels, to the general assembly and church of the first-born which are written in heaven, and to God the Judge of all, and to the spirits of just men made perfect, and to Jesus, the Mediator of the New Covenant, and to the blood of sprinkling that speaketh better things than that of Abel." (Heb. xii. 22.)

Even while he was thus discoursing, as they stood upon the bank of the *river*, two *shining ones*, with gentle pinions, were seen hovering over the dark waters, seeming to lighten up their gloom, and taking Probus by the hand, as he bade his friends farewell, flew gently over the *river* with him, amidst songs of welcome and great rejoicings, as they conducted him along a shining way, to a palace just short of the *Celestial City*, where he reposed for a brief period; and then, arrayed in a shining robe (Rev. vii. 9), was escorted up to the *Celestial City*, where he was receivd by the *Good Prince* and welcomed to the joys and privileges of the city as one who had not been ashamed to own and defend the cause of the *Prince*, amidst so many dangers and trials on the other side of the *river*.

His friends returned to their homes with solemn but chastened and happy hearts. (Eccl. vii. 2.) The report of *Probus's* departure soon got noised abroad, and his labors and passage over the *river* were the theme on every tongue. The current of thought and feeling thus turned for a season into such a profitable channel, it proved like good seed cast into good soil, and soon brought forth much fruit; and it was found that he slew by his death, even more than those he had in his life (Judges xvi. 31); for while in their grief for so great a loss, the virtues and strong faith of Probus were much talked of, even by those who had listened carelessly to his teaching, now seemed thoughtful and more interested than ever. And this reflection watered the good seed of truth sown in their minds, and scores came out and submitting to the gospel, at once set about preparing to go over the river and join him on the other side.

CHAPTER XX.

OBJECT AND USE OF DEATH—CONDITION AND STATES AFTER DEATH.

For all things are yours, whether the world, or life, or death, or things present or things to come, all are yours.—1 COR. iii. 21, 22.

UNFATHOMABLE are the ways of Jehovah, simply because of the shortness of our measuring line; mysterious too they may be, because our atmosphere is beclouded with the mists of sin and sense. But as the pathway of duty is made so clear in the blessed Scriptures to the willing mind that he that runs may read, so will the consistency and wisdom and harmony of all the ways of God appear in the light of eternity. And while a spirit of proper inquiry and desire to know is innocent and right, yet "secret things belong to God, while revealed things belong to us" (Deut. xxix. 29); so that to seek to become wise above what is written, is neither safe nor innocent. Life and death are terms of strange and mysterious import, bearing in their wondrous bosoms untold stores of joys and miseries, struggling in relentless strife, on every inch of the shore of time during every moment of its dominion, and throwing so dark a pall over the future, that it is only by *faith* in the divine revelation that we can take one step or see one inch of our pathway. We may not know the deep mystery of sin till our eyes have long been wonted to the orbless light of eternity. But since it is in the world, and the glorious problem of redemption from it has been brought out, let us be satisfied and rejoice in that inheritance to which death itself will contribute, together with all the present things of this world, if we but make a proper use of them, by releasing us from mortal clogs and qualifying us to enter a house not made with hands nor subject to decay. Thus mused *Clericus*, as arm in arm he and *Pilgrim* journeyed along the beautiful plain of Obedience in sweet converse about the ways of *Jehovah*, seemingly in full view of the Celestial City. But as they contemplated the river that rolled between them and the city, *Pilgrim* propounded this question—Why is it necessary for all to cross this dark river? Is there no other way to get to the city?

CLERICUS. Of course we are confined in our knowledge of these things to what the *Creator* has revealed to us in his word. Paul says (Heb. ix. 27) it was simply a divine appointment. The law under which man was placed when he was first made was, no doubt, founded in infinite wisdom, and embraced the principles of his being and happiness, the transgression of which brought misery and death.

PILGRIM. Do you mean to say naturally resulted in death?

CLERICUS. We use the term naturally in a somewhat ambiguous sense. Of course, he who made all law can control them as he pleases. Two men have been known to pass over the river without dying. And then, although death seems to follow sin as cause and effect, yet those whose sins are pardoned still die.

PILGRIM. May not the death threatened for sin be a different one from that of the body, while the body dies naturally?

CLERICUS. While it may be true that "the soul that sinneth, it shall die" (Ez. xviii. 4), yet the body, too, deprived of the tree of life (Gen. iii. 22), for the same reason dies. Hence even innocent ones die; and, by the same appointment, wicked ones and all will be brought up alive from the grave. (Jo. v. 28.)

PILGRIM. Then what is gained by making the body subject to death for a short period, if all are to be made alive?

CLERICUS. True, we may not see all that is gained —"secret things belong unto God." All the mysteries of redemption may be involved here. This earth seems to have been given to *Satan*. (Jo. xiv. 30.) And if man had been permitted to live always on this earth, under influences that most strongly inclined him to crimes, injustice, oppression, and licentiousness, no mind can conceive the black and terrible smoke of torment that would soon have ascended from every abode of man, mingled with wailing and gnashing of teeth.

PILGRIM. But if such be the result of sin, will it not still prove true? And why did Jehovah make man, or permit him to sin; and why not annihilate him and Satan too?

CLERICUS. Yes, such will be the fate of all who are not saved *from sin.* Your other questions I cannot answer. Yet gracious antidotes have been provided, so that all who will can be saved. (2 Pet. iii. 9.) The present state of man's being has been restricted. At first, he lived almost a thousand years, and the whole earth was filled with violence and blood (Gen. vi. 11); then one hundred years was a long life, and now more than one-half die in infancy, so that he is hindered as far as possible. No doubt the same reasons that produced man and Satan will forbid their annihilation, but require an end to this state.

PILGRIM. I remember, sir, this was one of the thoughts that first arrested my attention; and I also heard *Evangelist* say that God had appointed a day in which he would judge the world (Acts xvii. 31), and that all must then stand before the Judge (Rom. xiv. 10), to receive the things done in their bodies. Now, if the soul does not die with the body, and thus lie dormant till the judgment, what does become of them?

CLERICUS. Yes, and that judgment must be at the last day, or all cannot appear. As to the soul dying, the souls of the innocent and believing never die (Jo. iii. 36), but are, no doubt, in *Paradise,* a palace prepared this side the walls of the *Celestial City,* just across the river, while those of the wicked are in

Hades, or a dark region below *Paradise*, separated from it by a deep, impassable gulf. (Luke xvi. 26.)

PILGRIM. Ah! sir, this clears up these things to a great extent. Certainly, separated thus from the companionship of the wicked and the perverted, and clamoring appetites of the body, the saints must be still more happy and enjoy more of the presence of their Lord. (2 Cor. v. 8.)

CLERICUS. This, dear brother, is a solemn consideration. To be so devoted and attached to the Lord as to enjoy his service above all things else, is to find heaven wherever he is. If the cold-hearted and indifferent professor should tremble lest he find no such heaven, where shall the ungodly and sinner appear? (1 Pet. iv. 18.)

PILGRIM. True, clear views of what constitutes heaven and hell make many things plain. And if, instead of bothering about a thousand things that can be of no practical value to us, whether true or false, all were striving to attain to the pattern of Christ, heaven would be secured and all well. How strangely beautiful this path and the surrounding country appears. And although it seems near the close of the day yet the sun seems to shine clearer (Prov. iv. 18) and the air to be more balmy.

CLERICUS. Yes, dear brother, and the water from this river that still lies along our path, and the fruit of these trees seem sweeter, so that I feel a strange desire to go forward, even till we can pass the *dark river* that lies across our path. Nevertheless, such is the pleasure I now feel, that I could still remain in this delightful place. These beautiful lines have been running through my mind:

"We've no abiding city here,
We seek a city out of sight
Zion its name. We'll soon be there—
It shines with everlasting light.

"But hush, my soul, nor dare repine;
The time my God appoints is best.
While here, to do his will be mine,
And his to fix my time of rest."

PILGRIM. Ah! true, Brother Clericus. My own heart responds to these beautiful thoughts; and I was just thinking if the country along this *dark river* of death can be rendered so beautiful by a faithful, pious, holy journey, and even the passage of the river rendered so pleasant, death, after all, may not be much in the way of good men. Nay, rather it may be a blessed means of making him better off than he otherwise could be; and what the apostle says seems to imply as much—"All things shall work together for your good," for "all things are yours, whether life or death, or things present or things to come."

CLERICUS. It is very evident to my mind, since sin has marred the enjoyment of the present world, that we must exchange it for a better before we can be perfectly happy. And when we see what a wreck of hearts and hopes and expectations death causes here, what can be more precious than this increasing light you have noticed, and the fruit of these trees that grow along this river of life (Jo. iv. 14), which seems to gather these all up again, making for us a far more exceeding and eternal weight of glory and joy. Hence it was the apostle counted it all joy when he fell into temptation, and even gloried in tribulation. (Rom. v. 3.) For our bodies at last will be redeemed by the *Good Prince,* as well as our souls (Rom. viii. 23), and then, when this corruptible body puts on incorruption, and is again reunited to the soul, death will be swallowed up in everlasting victory.

The plain over which they were journeying, as it stretched away to the horizon on every hand, seemed more delightful than ever in the golden rays of the setting sun, for the day was now far spent. Bright streaks of glory shot aslant the dark river, revealing the dim outlines of the nether shore, thronged with joyous spirits, flitting to and fro in the silvery light, whereat *Pilgrim* could scarce restrain himself.

"Hark!" said he, "heard you not that glad note? Methinks I hear the heavenly arches ring, and I long to be with them. This glad hour more than makes amends for all the loss of the wages I met with when I gave up service in the city of Destruction—nay, makes the anxious hours and hard struggles and weary journey I have passed appear amazingly pleasant as I now look back."

CLERICUS. Yes! dear brother—

> "If such the sweetness of the stream
>   What must the fountain be,
> Where saints and angels draw their bliss
>   Immediately from *thee.*"

These notes you hear are the echoes in your own glad heart as you think of the past and anticipate the future, and these emotions rise ever in the hearts of the redeemed as new views of the works and ways of *Jehovah* are given to them. This raises their songs, and tunes their harps, and pours in one unceasing rapture through their souls, swelling and echoing over the everlasting hills.

But see, there is a group of friends watching us from yonder enticing home by the way-side; let us join them, as the day is near spent.

So they drew near, and were at once welcomed to a pleasant Christian home by the inmates, who had learned to take delight in entertaining all strangers that came along this *plain.*

And after a most delightful repast, their host, noticing that they were weary, called the hour of evening worship early, and then directed *Sympathy*, the chamberlain, to conduct them to the chamber of *Promise*, for therein reposed all who journeyed over the Plain of *Obedience*, which chamber was in full view of the *Celestial City*.

CHAPTER XXI.

PASSAGE OF THE RIVER—ARRIVAL AT THE CELESTIAL CITY.

Then shall be brought to pass the saying that is written, Death is swallowed up in victory.—1 Cor. xv. 54.

Wearied and feeble as they were from the length of their journey, yet their sleep was sweet and refreshing. So long had they dwelt upon the love of the *Good Prince*, in giving his life for the salvation of sinners, and the many infallible proofs that, though dead, he was alive again forevermore, and held the keys of death and hell (Rev. i. 18); so often had they revolved the promise in their mind, "As I live ye shall live also," together with other reasons of the hope that was within them, that all these things came up in their dreams, so that the spirit seemed wakeful and soaring while the flesh grew weak.

So, when the morning came, with its usual salutations and refreshments and worship, they would fain go forward; but so pleasant seemed the intercourse of these newly-made friends, that the time flew swiftly by in sweet converse about the heavenly land, the wondrous love of Him who could leave so bright a world with such kingly honors, and princely wealth, and ecstatic pleasures in angelic company, unmarred by sin or sinners, to come down to poverty and sorrow, and buffeting and desertion, and finally the most painful death, in order that He might redeem and bless those who would thus treat Him and ruin themselves. Indeed, so earnest were their friends, that *Clericus* and *Pilgrim* consented to tarry a few days, that they might rest themselves a little and feast their souls on these delightful themes.

Now, said *Clericus*, addressing the host, it seems to me your countenance is familiar, and, from the manner in which you and your good lady, with the members of your household, seem to anticipate our wants, and so exactly meet them, that I have been your guest before.

HOST. Very likely. My name is *Grace*, and my companion's *Charity*, and we have long been living on these *plains*, by the order of our *Prince*, to provide for and comfort pilgrims, whom it is our greatest pleasure to serve. And as we usually have a surplus of provisions, we frequently make journeys along the King's highway, to distribute them to any travellers that may need.

PILGRIM. Did we not see thee in *Berea?*

MR. GRACE. Without doubt. We have been there much, and with *Mr. Evangelist* often, and all along the road.

PILGRIM. The same, and I wondered why we should feel so much at home. And, Brother Clericus, I have been thinking, as memory is somewhat fading, whether we should know any of our friends when we get across the river.

CLERICUS. Without doubt. Did not Peter, James

and John know Moses and Elias, and Dives recognize Lazarus. Did not Stephen and John recognize the Saviour? and does not the Revelator tell us the martyred saints remembered their persecutions on the earth, and that their sins had been washed away? and does not the apostle tell us we shall receive for the things done while in the body? Certainly, we shall not only remember these and one another, but we shall recognize those about whom we have thought much, as Abraham, Isaac and Jacob, Moses, Daniel and the Saviour. It is this knowledge of personal identity and consciousness that will there, as here, constitute much of our pleasure.

HOST. True, brethren; and if these things be so, those who have made most friends and done most good here, will be most happy there, while those who have many enemies, or have not done and sacrificed much to save others, will not have much to enjoy, if they should happen to get to the Celestial City, if they are not made very unhappy when they reflect upon those sufferings and pangs of everlasting torment which they might have saved.

PILGRIM. Dear brethren, when so near the river, and the bright land beyond seems so inviting that I long to be there, yet now I am in a strait betwixt two (Phil. i. 23), for it seems to me if I could live my life over again, I would try and give more to the cause of Christ and labor more to save others, that the happiness of each might be increased by the addition of all.

CHARITY. Truly this is a proper spirit, for while

thus we feel our own hearts burning with love for others, we see what actuated the *Blessed One* to lay down his life for us, and we shall need to remember all when we come into His presence, that we may know how to say, "Thou art worthy to receive honor, and dominion, and glory, for thou hast redeemed us by thy blood."

While thus discoursing, as they sat in the chamber of *Promise*, they seemed to have a full view of the *city* across the river; and behold three *shining ones* appeared coming over toward them. And as they drew near, their presence seemed to fill the room with light. And after some tokens of satisfaction and approbation from the *King*, they presented a message, summoning *Clericus* and *Pilgrim* over the river. Whereat, the two travellers, with the aid of this kind household, began to get ready to go over. The sun was gently sinking in the western horizon as they all went together down to the river, when behold, a light from the *city* seemed to fade the golden rays of the setting sun by its superior beauty.

Pilgrim bade his friends an affectionate farewell and turned to enter the *river*, while *Clericus* seemed inclined to linger a little, with many exhortations and prayers and tears, urging them to be faithful and active still in blessing others and getting them ready to cross the river; then, bidding them a warm adieu, he followed on, Pilgrim going a little before.

Now, as they gently and safely passed the river, the waters seemed to separate hither and thither. And as they ascended the opposite banks, a flaming chariot and horses of fire, sent by *Immanuel* (Jo. xiv. 3), took them up, while all the bank and road leading up from thence to the city was thronged with happy spirits who had gone before (Heb. xii. 23) clothed in white, with palms in their hands, intermingled with angels, welcoming them and conducting them along the shining way to the celestial Paradise. (Luke xvi. 22.) But, oh! how joyful; never had they been so happy before. The joy of their first consecration when on arising from the waters of baptism, and hearing the voice of the Saviour's *promise* of *pardon*, and receiving his Holy Spirit of *adoption*, seemed renewed, overflowing. And there, standing out in bold relief, away up, up on the Mount of God, stood the *Celestial City*, the end of all their toils and desires, with its high walls all ablaze with brilliants and waving banners.

The weight of glory seemed almost oppressive. And eager as their excited spirits were to go on, yet they were glad when a shining messenger announced that it was the King's pleasure that they might remain a little season to recover and familiarize themselves with this heavenly land.

During this interval, how vivid was their recollection of the past! Every unkind word, every harsh and wicked act, every unimproved opportunity, all came in swift review. And had not such sayings as these come to remembrance—"He came not to call the righteous, but sinners, to repentance;" "According to His mercy, he saved us by the washing of regeneration and renewing of the Holy Spirit"—they would, in despair, have turned back. But now the mysteries of redemption and depths of redeeming love gradually unfolding before their minds, filled them with new wonder and courage.

So, when the messengers again returned to escort them to the city, they submitted to their guidance, when a multitude that no man can number seemed moving with them, the spirits of those who had gone before cheering and rejoicing with them, while the shining ones told them of the glorious city, its gold-paved streets and pearly gates, its wondrous temple, and ever-flowing river of life, whose banks were lined with "*arbor vitæ*," whose never-fading leaves and never-failing fruit, afforded food and shelter; of the robes of white that never waxed old; of sweet music on golden harps touched by instinctive fingers; of glad intercourse with pure and holy ones, free from all guile and misunderstanding; and, above all, the presence and smile of the King in his beauty, which was a constant feast to the soul.

"There no alternate night is known
Nor sun's faint, sickly ray
But glory from the eternal throne
Spreads everlasting day.

"No chilling winds nor poïs'nous breath
Can reach that healthful shore;
Sickness and sorrow, pain and death,
Are felt and feared no more."

Ascending thus, in sweet discourse, along the ambient way, when lo! the King himself was seen descending, with ten thousand of his saints. "His garment was white as snow, and the hair of his head like pure wool; his throne was like the fiery flame, and his wheels as burning fire; a fiery stream issued and came forth from before him; thousands of thousands ministered unto him, and ten thousand times ten thousand stood before him." (Dan. vii. 9, 10.) And now, being informed who these two newly come were, and learning of their obedience to his orders (2 Thess. i. 10), and faithfulness in following his directions (2 Pet. i. 11), also welcomed them to his train, and, returning to the city, there presented them to the Almighty Father. (Matt. x. 32.) Now, as they entered the gates, they were clothed with those shining garments, which transformed them like unto the angels. They also had crowns put upon their heads, and palms in their hands, to wave in signal of triumph, while a strange, soft, swelling sound arose from the sea-like multitude before them, saying, "Enter ye into the joy of your Lord." (Matt. xxv. 23.) Then a golden harp was given to each of them, and, as the anthem swelled again, they joined in it, saying, "Blessing and honor, and glory and power, be unto Him that sitteth upon the throne, and unto the Lamb for ever and ever." (Rev. v. 13.)

All that had been told them of the beauty and glory of the city was more than realized. Great was their joy at finding *Probus* and *Resolute,* and many other dear ones, with whom they had lived and loved and toiled in the blessed service of the Master on the other side of the river, unto whom the King addressed himself, giving them free permission to walk the gold-paved streets, or range the flowing plains, to drink of the river, and eat of the fruit that grew on its banks, and repose in heavenly mansions. Here, too, said he, all the toil-worn ones of earth, sick of sin and panting for deliverance, the bereaved and heart-broken, shall meet again; even all that have taken delight in my ways shall here find the desire of their hearts and dwell in this *Celestial City* for ever; while new joys and beauties will unceasingly unfold before them.

"Oh! sweet abode of peace and love,
Where pilgrims, freed from toil, are blest!
Had I the pinions of a dove,
I'd fly to thee, and be at rest."

THE END.

www.ingramcontent.com/pod-product-compliance
Lightning Source LLC
LaVergne TN
LVHW011205110826
845150LV00006B/1325
* 9 7 8 1 4 2 5 5 1 8 7 8 3 *